Bullied and Teased or Just Another Kid?

Bullied and Teased or Just Another Kid?

The Social Experiences of
Students with Disabilities at School

JUDE MACARTHUR AND MICHAEL GAFFNEY

NEW ZEALAND COUNCIL FOR EDUCATIONAL RESEARCH
Wellington 2001

New Zealand Council for Educational Research
Box 3237, Wellington, New Zealand

© Jude MacArthur & Michael Gaffney 2001

ISBN 1-877293-04-0

All rights reserved.

Distributed by NZCER Distribution Services
PO Box 3237, Wellington, New Zealand
www.nzcer.org.nz

Contents

Introduction		7
Chapter 1:	An Introduction to the Social Experiences of Children with Disabilities at School	9
Chapter 2:	Students' Experiences of Bullying	19
Chapter 3:	Students' Friendships and Relationships	51
Chapter 4:	Siblings, Bullying and Friendships	83
Chapter 5:	Implications for Schools: Creating Safe and Supportive School Environments for Students with Disabilities and their Siblings	93
References		106
Index		112

Dedication

This book is dedicated to the children, young people and their parents who have willingly shared their experiences with us and with those who read this book. There is a personal cost to recounting difficult stories. We hope that this book will be a form of repayment, by contributing to practices that make schools better places for all children.

Introduction

The research project described in this book looked at the social experiences of a group of students with disabilities in primary and secondary schools. Our original aim was to investigate whether bullying was a problem for children with disabilities; and if so, to explore strategies to address the problem. There is growing evidence that bullying is a worldwide problem (Adair, 1999). New Zealand is no exception, with one of the highest youth suicide rates in the world, some of which can be attributed to bullying (Sullivan, 2000). In recent years, the age-old phenomenon of bullying at school has re-emerged as a major issue affecting children's safety, well-being and healthy development.

With the increasing trend to include children with disabilities in ordinary classrooms and schools, it is important that we know about their experiences of school, particularly their relationships with peers. Bullying has been shown to have serious and often long-term effects on children's mental health, and may be particularly harmful for children with disabilities. There are some suggestions that students with disabilities may be vulnerable to bullying, particularly where the focus is on difference, but little is known about what really happens in schools.

We recognised, however, that bullying happens in a wider social context. Students with disabilities can have unusual social experiences at school which are characterised by loneliness and a lack of friends (MacArthur and Morton, 1999; Traustadottir, 1993). This may make them particularly vulnerable to bullying. Nurturing and sustaining social relationships, on the other hand, are critical to children's overall development and learning, and may also serve as a protection against bullying. Friendships at any age are at the heart of what is needed to ensure a high quality of life. On this basis, the project extended beyond a study of bullying to include children's relationships and friendships at school. It involved a collaborative, interdisciplinary team of researchers with backgrounds in health and education from the Children's Issues Centre (Professor Anne Smith, Michael Gaffney and Megan Gollop) and the Donald Beasley Institute (Jude MacArthur and Anne Bray).

The project aimed to contribute to the increasing international literature on relationships and bullying, by looking in particular at the perspectives and experiences of students with disabilities and their families. It is hoped that this book will help teachers and others to understand children's social experiences at school, including their experience of bullying and the context in which it happens, and to develop welcoming and safe school environments for children with disabilities.

We would like to thank the children, young people and their parents who volunteered to participate in this project. Their stories are important because they add to the knowledge and understandings that we as researchers and teachers can bring to the issues of relationships and bullying. The project was supported by funding from Otago Research Grants, University of Otago, and from the Child Protection Otago Trust. The project was reviewed and approved by the University of Otago Research and Ethics Committee. We gratefully acknowledge the support of these groups.

Dr Jude MacArthur
Donald Beasley Institute
P.O. Box 6189
DUNEDIN
jude.macarthur@stonebow.otago.ac.nz

Michael Gaffney
Children's Issues Centre,
University of Otago
P.O. Box 56, DUNEDIN
michael.gaffney@stonebow.otago.ac.nz

CHAPTER 1
An Introduction to the Social Experiences of Children with Disabilities at School

Friendships, relationships and children with disabilities

Friendships are an important feature of children's lives, and become increasingly important as children reduce their dependence on family relationships for their social well-being. Smith (1998a) lists seven components of friendship: proximity, shared activities, similar attitudes and values, tangible support offered between friends, intimacy and self-disclosure, trust, and reciprocity. This list suggests that establishing and maintaining friendships is a socially complex task for any child. As children spend so much of their time in schools, the school setting becomes a critical social context for the development of friendships. It is no different for children with disabilities.

While the achievement objectives in the Health and Physical Education Curriculum include a focus on relationships, personal identity and self-worth, the development of friendships may not always be an explicit component of the daily curriculum in New Zealand schools. So the question needs to be asked: will children with disabilities develop friendships without adult intervention, as we might assume is the case for children without disabilities? Parents are quick to point out that the social experiences of their sons and daughters with disabilities are often different from those of their siblings and peers, and to make a plea for them to have the opportunity to be 'an ordinary kid' (Purdue, MacArthur and Ballard, 1998). Without friends, isolation itself is disabling. As well as having a negative impact on quality of life, isolation heightens the vulnerability to abuse experienced by children and adults with disabilities (Strully and Strully, 1992).

Reciprocal friendships do occur between people with disabilities and those without, both in schools and in other community settings (Amado, 1993; Bogdan and Taylor, 1992; Lutfiyya, 1990; Murray-Seegert, 1989; Taylor and Bogdan, 1989). Such friendships and supportive relationships are less likely to grow when students with disabilities are not present in mainstream settings, or are present only intermittently (Schnorr, 1990). Yet even when students with disabilities are part of the regular classroom for most, if not all, of the school day, it is still possible for them to be 'islands in the mainstream' (Sapon-Shevin et al., 1998, p.105). Meyer et al. (1998, p.203) describe 'facades of friendship', where the student with a disability is labelled by staff and peers as 'the inclusion kid', or experiences relationships where the emphasis is almost entirely on their being helped. In a study of primary school children, Salisbury and Palombaro (1998) observed a range of relationships between children, from unequal relationships characterised by too much help and too much attention, through to equal and respectful relationships that recognised children's needs for both interdependence and independence.

Recent literature on friendships for children and young people with disabilities urges parents and professionals to begin by familiarising themselves with the natural evolution of children's friendships (Salisbury and Palombaro, 1998; Sapon-Shevin et al., 1998). Yet the child development literature on children's friendships through preschool, primary and secondary school (e.g. Smith, 1998a) issues some challenges to those interested in supporting friendships between disabled and non-disabled students, particularly with regard to the competencies involved in friendship development. For example, children with disabilities may find it difficult to engage in reciprocal or mutual exchanges in the traditional sense (Salisbury and Palombaro, 1998). For some students with more significant disabilities, it may be difficult or impossible to achieve other behaviours associated with making friends, such as giving attention, approval and affection, complying with others' wishes, giving things to others, being able to communicate accurately, and being good at something that other children value (Smith, 1998a).

The impact of these challenges on the development of friendships and social relationships is not well understood. Nonetheless, Zetlin and Murtaugh (1988) and Hall (1994) have found that, contrary to the expectations of some teaching staff, friendships do develop between students with disabilities and those without, and that some of these friendships are high in intimacy and empathy as well as long lasting. On this basis, Salisbury and Palombaro (1998, p.82) suggest that 'studying the relationships between children without disabilities and their classmates with significant disabilities may lead to understanding how and why certain friendships emerge, what sustains them, and how they might differ from acquaintance relationships'.

In their qualitative study of three such friendships in an inclusive primary school, Salisbury and Palombaro (1998) conclude that increased levels of physical, social and instructional inclusion occur when teachers and support staff create caring and supportive classroom environments, based on a philosophy that 'everyone belongs', as well as providing the time and opportunity to interact. They also observed adults children to become socially aware, and giving them ∍sses and skills to act on their new knowledge of the cniid with a disability (e.g. learning how to communicate with that child).

Salisbury and Palombaro (1998) stress the need to re-examine the traditional markers of friendship and to seek out 'more robust boundaries to capture the nontraditional nature of interactions among peers in inclusive classrooms' (p.101). The focus of education, they suggest, should be on 'building supportive social environments rather than on developing friendships per se' among students (p.102).

Bullying and children with disabilities

In New Zealand, increasing numbers of children with disabilities are being included in regular classrooms. It might be expected that children with more severe disabilities would be more likely to be bullied because of their marked differences, yet the research evidence (e.g. Evans et al., 1992) suggests that they attract nurturing behaviour or are ignored, rather than being bullied. In contrast, children with mild or moderate disabilities are more likely to be bullied, with teasing and name-calling extremely common (Mooney and Smith, 1995). Interviews with adults with disabilities who were bullied at school show the devastating and often long-term effects of such behaviour (Ballard, 1998; Mooney and Smith, 1995). There is, however, very little research that asks children about their experiences while they are still at school.

Torrance (2000) has recently published a review of the issues faced by researchers working in this area. One study that did interview children was by Whitney et al. (1994), as part of a major research project into school bullying in the UK (Smith and Sharp, 1994). It found that more children with disab were bullied than non-disabled children; they were bu more frequently; and they were more likely to be involved in bullying others. Much of the bullying they experienced was related to their special needs. Teachers underestimated whether, and how often, children with disabilities were being bullied, particularly in primary and intermediate schools. The research also showed the effectiveness of school-based intervention strategies in reducing bullying.

The study by Whitney et al. focused on children in special classes, so we do not know whether inclusion in regular classes increases or decreases children's experiences of bullying. Torrance (1997), on the other hand, focused her study on a single mainstream classroom, where 19 of the 25 eleven- and twelve-year-olds reported that they had been bullied. Six of these children were deemed to have 'special educational needs', and all six said they had been bullied away from the school. They did not indicate that bullying was a big problem at school, yet their peers identified them as being victims of bullying, particularly through exclusion. Torrance attributes this to the possibility that students with special needs may not equate social isolation with 'active bullying'.

In New Zealand, representative school populations have been surveyed on the subject of bullying (Adair et al., 1998; Maxwell and Lind, 1996). Yet there have been few in-depth interview studies that include family perspectives, and none to our knowledge that have focused on children with disabilities. Our project set out to explore this under-researched area by asking those most directly affected – the children themselves, and their siblings and parents.

Definitions of bullying used in the study

The term 'bullying' is used to cover a wide range of behaviours, all of which cause hurt to the victim without the perpetrator having any fear of retaliation. Sullivan (2000, p.9) describes bullying as 'a conscious and wilful act of aggression and/or manipulation by one or more people against another person or people'. It can be short or long term, and represents an abuse of power by those who carry it out. According to Sullivan, bullying contains the following elements: 'harm is intended; there is an imbalance of power; it is often organised or systematic; it is repetitive or random; and hurt experienced by the victim may be either physical or psychological' (pp.9-10). We have used Sullivan's definitions to describe the different forms of bullying experienced by students in our study:

Physical bullying – includes biting, hair-pulling, hitting, kicking, locking in a room, pinching, poking, pushing, scratching, spitting, or other forms of physical attack. It also includes damaging a person's property.

Non-physical bullying – can be verbal or non-verbal, and includes intimidation or threats of violence, name-calling, racist (and we would add 'disablist') remarks or teasing, sexually suggestive or abusive language, spiteful teasing or cruel remarks, and spreading false or malicious rumours.

The approach

Our study focused on the social experiences of a group of primary and secondary school students who have disabilities. For this book we have selected examples that highlight important issues relating to friendships, isolation and bullying. The children's perspectives in particular reveal aspects of their school experience which might otherwise remain invisible, if not to parents then certainly to teachers. We explore some of the features of the school context that might be associated with bullying and social isolation, and those that might be associated with more nurturing and pro-social behaviour towards children with disabilities.

The project was qualitative, and relied on semi-structured, in-depth interviews to solicit the participants' meanings and understandings about the children's social experiences at school. An interpretivist approach aims to understand the complex world of lived experience from the point of view of those who live it (Schwandt, 1994). It also enables the meanings and interpretations of the key actors (the students and parents in our study) to be studied without too many constraints from the researchers' preconceived categories.

This was a promising way of identifying the interplay between the causal and interpretive perspectives so central to understanding the key issues in this debate, and allowed a narrative to emerge from the varying perspectives (Cresswell, 1994). In a recent reinterpretation of bullying as 'intimidatory practices', Maharaj et al. (2000) argue for the addition of a socio-cultural context to the study of bullying, suggesting that studies of intimidatory practices should adopt a more inclusive research perspective that is multi-dimensional. Studies need to be empirical and interpretive, 'dealing with the inter-subjective nature of meaning as well as its personalised, subjective dimension'. Children's experiences at school are 'filled with both "meaning" and "meaningfulness" and any attempt to represent them in their fullness requires a range of investigatory procedures' (p.19).

The participants

Eleven children with disabilities and their parents and siblings were recruited from families belonging to a formal support group and by advertising in a community newspaper. Participation was voluntary, with rights of confidentiality, anonymity and withdrawal assured. All but one of the children were in mainstream classrooms for the entire school day. One secondary school student was taught in a special unit on a secondary school site.

The participants comprised:
- eleven students with a disability (ranging in age from seven to fifteen), 10 boys and 1 girl. All students were able to communicate their experiences to the interviewer
- eleven siblings of the children with disabilities (families were selected where the sibling was as close as possible in age to the child with a disability; in all cases, the sibling was either currently at or had previously been at the same school as the child with a disability)
- eleven sets of parents.

The interviews

Interviews with parents were the first to be scheduled. These explored their children's development and educational history and experience, including their friendships and relationships with other children at home and at school. Parents were also asked to describe any incidents of bullying they had encountered, the school's response, and the eventual outcome. The researchers thus gained some knowledge of the child's disability, any communication problems they might have, and the most appropriate way to determine the child's perspective.

Interviews with the children with disabilities and their

siblings were carried out by interviewers from the Children's Issues Centre and the Donald Beasley Institute who had experience of working with children. Since friendship and bullying are sensitive issues, it was important to approach them carefully. The interview schedule prompted questions on subjects ranging from the child's family through to friendships, relationships and bullying. During the early part of the interview, a video or books were used to encourage the child to talk generally about bullying in the context of some fictional examples (see Box). The interviewer then moved on to ask the child how they had been treated at school. The child was asked to think about their recent experiences at school in relation to their social interactions with peers.

Motivational material

The books used as prompts during the children's interviews to raise issues about bullying included:

> Morpurgo, M. (1988) *Who's a big bully then?* Edinburgh: Barrington Stoke
> Hofmann, G. (1996) *The big bully bear.* New York: Random House
> Nimmo, J. and Howard, P. (1999) *Esmeralda and the children-next-door.* Mascot, NSW: Koala Books
> Hughes, D. (1993) *Bully.* London: Walker Books
> Browne, A. (1992) *Willy and Hugh.* London: Red Fox Books
> Wilhelm, H. (1988) *Tyrone the horrible.* London: Scholastic
> The video used in the interviews was:
> New Zealand Police Law Related Education Programme (1995) *Kia Kaha: A resource kit about bullying for students, teachers and parents. For Standard 3 – Form 4.* Wellington: New Zealand Police.

All of the interviews, except one, were tape-recorded and then transcribed. The analysis of the data involved the research team reading and deriving categories from interview transcripts. These were coded and classified to reflect the salient issues for participants and the questions that initiated and structured the study (Pitman and Maxwell, 1992). No real names are used in this book, and any potentially identifying features have been removed.

CHAPTER 2
Students' Experiences of Bullying

'We've got an absence of tolerance' (Scott, aged fourteen)
'Probably it's because I'm a disability' (Tom, aged eight)

What's happening, who's doing what and why?

The experiences of the students, their parents and their siblings provided some important insights into the social processes surrounding bullying, which involved both students and teachers. Sullivan (2000) points out that bullies come in all shapes and sizes, as do victims. By improving their understanding of bullying, schools and communities will be better equipped to deal effectively with all its various forms. The children and parents we talked to have alerted us to some of the ways in which schools can either contribute to or challenge bullying.

Of the eleven children we interviewed, nine had recent or past experience of bullying at school. Yet overall, the experiences of the families covered a wide range. For some children with disabilities, isolation, loneliness and bullying were ongoing issues with few obvious solutions. For others, a change of school had brought new hopes for friendship, and a supportive environment in which bullying simply did not happen. Some parents were engaged in an ongoing and generally supportive dialogue with their child's school in an attempt to address issues relating to friendship and bullying as they arose. For these families the issues were often complex and worrying, and the search for solutions required a certain amount of energy and tenacity.

Four students had experienced physical bullying, ranging from having their school-bag snatched away through to specific incidents of hitting, kicking and serious threats. In most cases, the school viewed physical bullying as a serious matter and took immediate action to stop it. All of the nine students had experienced non-physical bullying, most commonly name-calling and teasing. While most schools appeared to have well-understood strategies in place for both students and teachers to deal with bullying, it persisted nonetheless in some places.

This reinforces the point made by Sullivan (2000) that bullying is more widespread than most people realise. The students with disabilities, their parents and their siblings described examples of persistent bullying, both overt and covert, which often went unseen by teachers and which caused considerable anxiety for the whole family. Girls were commonly identified as the perpetrators of bullying at primary school. Often the bullied students did not have close friends who might offer some protection; but where they did have friends they provided an important safety net. Several of the bullied students felt that the bullying was personal and directed at them because they were different and/or vulnerable.

Eight-year-old Tom, who has a physical disability, was bullied at his primary school. When asked what he liked least about school, he replied: 'getting picked on...the bullies [who] push me over and hit me in the head with a skipping rope.' One girl 'threatened to hit me in the back if I didn't give her my fish and chips', and Tom decided the best strategy was to comply with her demands 'because I didn't want to make it worse'. He described being 'kicked and punched in the back all [through] assembly' by girls, and ending up crying. Tom's mother knew of incidents where he had been 'tied up with skipping ropes and flax, and pushed and shoved', particularly by girls. The school had arranged for one girl to be assigned a teacher aide to support her for other reasons, but this had the effect of preventing her from bullying, and her physical attacks had been reduced to 'giving the evil eye'.

Tom's mother recognised that bullies were 'not happy in their own life', and Tom himself described one perpetrator as 'very sad...[in a] foster home'. He also acknowledged that his disability made him vulnerable:

Interviewer: Have you got any idea why some kids pick on other kids?
Tom: Probably it's because I'm a disability and probably because I don't know what really to do [in] that sort of situation because these kids are in big gangs...

Interestingly, Tom's interpretation contrasted with that of Martin, the nine-year-old brother of AJ, aged twelve, who has a disability:

Interviewer: What about AJ? Has he ever been teased?
Martin: No, like everyone in the school likes him.
Interviewer: OK, why is that do you reckon?
Martin: Hmm, I don't know, because he's got a disability.

In this case, AJ's sense of humour may have been an important mediating factor in his relationships with other children:

Interviewer: Is he good at making other kids laugh?
Martin: Yeah ... everyone cracks up [with him].
Interviewer: What sorts of things does he do?
Martin: Just hands in his pockets and goes [spinning his arms and body around and falling over] and his arms go in circles and everybody cracks up at that.

Aidan, a secondary student with an intellectual disability, was being taught in a special unit at secondary school, and was physically bullied by other students in the unit. Aidan's mother described the place as 'becoming a dumping ground for [students with] behaviour problems, social problems... and my son was suffering because of it'. When asked about the nature of the bullying, she replied:

> Oh, just thumping, physical, you know, thumping and kicking, he had bruises all over him...I've seen it in front of my own eyes inside the unit...as if you can call it a safe place, sometimes I think it's the unsafest place. But I think Aidan would still refer to it as a safe place because it's the place he's got to know...

Aidan's mother raised the issue with the school, and some of the perpetrators were 'moved on'. Her response was a mixture of discomfort and relief:

> I've kicked up about bullying so much this year that three that came into the unit this year have gone, they've been moved on...you shouldn't have to as a parent be going down there and saying 'well, this one's picking on that one'...it got to the stage where I was worried about his safety, and then the worst one out of the lot was gone.

However, Aidan's mother felt that most students in the school were very supportive of students with disabilities:

> One day some students brought Aidan into the office [after he had fallen] and one had given him his Walkman for a while because he was concerned about Aidan being upset.

It was most notable that the bullies were students who had not grown up with or attended school with the student who had a disability. Scott, a fifteen-year-old with an autism spectrum disability and a high academic achiever was teased mostly by third- and fourth-formers who had come from different primary and intermediate schools. For Scott, this had been true of every school he had attended. His mother commented:

> When he was at primary school, it was always the kids who came to the school who had never known him previously who would start to make fun of him – kids that never knew him before or [hadn't] grown up with him. Or, when he was at Intermediate, there were lots of kids that never knew him before, so he had suddenly become the butt of something. Whereas other kids who knew him just accepted that was him. That was just Scott.

Bullying at primary and intermediate school had been a serious issue for Scott and his family. Other children terrorised him by playing on his fears, and also teased him about wearing glasses. Scott described himself at this stage as 'suicidal, trying to mutilate myself'. Teachers also made the mistake of 'lumping him together' with another student who had an intellectual disability and assigning them both the same teacher aide:

Mother: Scott felt, yeah, it was sheep and goats…he felt he was being classified along with this student as a 'dummy'. I mean, that's an awful way of putting it but that was his perception…they had very different needs…yet it reinforced an assumption that they were the same, and some kids even called Scott by this other student's name.

Scott was much happier at secondary school, and felt that he had 'adapted over time' to dealing more effectively with name-calling. He was embarrassed by the names some third- and fourth-formers called him, and did not even like to tell his parents about incidents at school. Scott asked his mother to initiate the conversation about name-calling:

Mother:	I think Scott is feeling a bit embarrassed about what they called him...it was something homophobic, can you tell Megan at all?
Scott:	Well, they continued teasing and harassing me, and of course I could not see a clear way around the difficulty anyway, because there was a problem...I was not going out in the rain. Well, I found their behaviour intolerable, so I told.
Mother:	It was lunchtime, and it was raining and you were inside by yourself, weren't you?
Scott:	Yes, always.
Mother:	And some little third-formers who had some nasty rumours told to them about Scott...started to call him these names. He was on his own and they teased him about being on his own, didn't they?
Scott:	Yes.
Mother:	They see him around on his own so they teased him about that as well. Now Scott didn't actually tell anyone about this...
Interviewer:	So how did you feel about it all, what was your reaction?
Scott:	Well, I didn't react to it. I thought of it as pathetic and so I simply walked past, sat and ignored it...It's quite offensive, some of it.

Like other students in the study, Scott found that name-calling was most likely to occur when others were not around to hear it and intervene. Scott felt that most teasing was directed at people who were 'different', suggesting that 'we've got an absence of tolerance'. He believed that, for some students, the cause was internal:

...some are just, well, personalities, there are some terrible personalities...[they are] pressured, not able to, well, obviously not able to prevent themselves so that seems to be the only way they're able to express themselves.

Ryan, a seven-year-old with a physical disability, was also teased by children who did not know him well, and particularly by girls from a different part of the school: 'They say I'm too skinny, and not strong enough to play games like soccer, and they are strong or something.' Ryan's mother felt that he was 'very confident in his own class, he feels tremendous support from this group' who knew and understood him. Ryan's mother and Ryan himself had been instrumental in ensuring that other students in the class understood his disability. His teachers had been supportive in reinforcing their messages, although the transient nature of the class made it difficult to keep all the children informed.

Ryan's main concern was the girls from another part of the school who, according to his mother:

...sort of look at him, whispering, giggling, this sort of stuff. He's noticed very much that it's girls that seem to do that when he's entering a new group, and not boys, and I must say I've noticed that too...he's very anti-girls at the moment.

More recently, there had been some examples of teasing within Ryan's own class. He had told his mother that when the class plays 'Octopus' in PE he gets particularly upset, because:

...he feels he can't run as fast as the others and he gets caught more often...he cries and the teacher's very supportive. I mean, he often takes himself off...calms himself down and then he comes back into the group and the teacher helps him to do that without too much fuss...but some of the girls purposely try to catch him rather than going for others, because they see he is anxious...it's like 'Let's get Ryan because he doesn't really like this'. He gets really upset...I don't know what their motivation is...

Ryan's mother worried that the subtle and sometimes complex issues around teasing, particularly by girls, were not always easy for teachers to detect. She had raised some concerns with Ryan's teacher about this teasing:

> [The girls] know these little vulnerable things he feels...it's almost a bit of a sport to wind Ryan up...we've raised the issue with the teachers but we need to talk about it in more depth because [the bullying is] sort of subtle and it's not always obvious and I think Ryan feels that perhaps he's blamed and the girls are always right and the boys are the baddies and the girls are the goodies.

Mike, a secondary student with physical and learning difficulties, had been physically bullied at primary school. His mother described some of the incidents:

> [He had] a dead bird pushed down his shirt, he was spat on, hit with a brick, and his pants were pulled down. His glasses were broken or snapped in half many times...I once found him at school screaming in the toilets. Two children had 'bumped into him' in the toilet, either accidentally or on purpose, I'm not sure...

She felt the prevailing attitude in the school was that Mike was 'whingeing', and that 'this kind of thing doesn't happen here'. This meant that the bullying was not always adequately dealt with, a situation that is discussed in the following section.

Leah, a twelve-year-old with low vision and other disabilities, had no experience of bullying at her small rural primary school. This was because clear boundaries were established, and Leah's mother felt that in this school 'the kids just wouldn't think to do that sort of thing'. Now that she was at intermediate school, it was the students who didn't know her that were involved in teasing: 'In the first few weeks, [they were] encouraging her to lift skirts and chase other kids with her cane, things like that.'

Leah's disability made it difficult for her to interpret these actions as inappropriate:

> Leah tells me what she's been up to because I always like to talk to the kids about how the day's been. I'm not sure how else I could have heard about it. The teacher's aide, I think, might have spotted it too. I immediately raised [the issue] because I have very good open communication with the teacher, and it was addressed. I understand the class was spoken to about it – about expectations for their behaviour in this school, and about the importance of modelling appropriate behaviour for Leah...[Teasing] comes from a lack of understanding about disability...the kids who have come through with Leah [from primary school], it would never enter their heads to tease her; it's the kids who don't know her [who bully]. This is why inclusive education is so important. It proves it. I mean she's a living testament that you get them in there and get those kids around her.

Leah's mother acted on behalf of her daughter by telling the teacher, and the issues were immediately addressed. She realised that Leah was an easy target for bullying because she did not have a good understanding of what was appropriate or inappropriate behaviour at school:

> She doesn't really get that upset about bullying because she hasn't got that level of understanding that she's actually being teased. It's interesting because she can come home and say, 'Mum, I have feelings'. I say, 'What kind of feelings do you have?', and she'll say, 'Well, just a bit mixed up about what's happening'. She's not able to express herself but she is starting to twig that she's different, because we've always brought her up to see that everybody's different and she's been spared from any really rough stuff...she has no concept that it's not appropriate.

Leah's experience reinforces the need for teachers to be particularly sensitive to the impact of a student's disability on their social experiences at school. It also underlines the critical importance of drawing on parents' knowledge of their child when seeking solutions to isolation and bullying.

School contexts that were unresponsive to reports of bullying

While some families felt that schools had taken their concerns on board and responded to them, others felt frustrated and powerless to improve their situation. Three families had changed schools as a direct result of a school failing to address their concerns about bullying, and one of those families was looking at another change of school.

Some schools responded to issues of bullying in ways that seemed to perpetuate rather than confront the problem. In such schools, the problem was denied or the complaint dismissed; the victim was blamed; teachers were not always available for support; or teachers simply did not respond to reports of bullying.

That sort of thing doesn't happen here...

Some schools seemed unsure about how to respond to parents' and children's reports of bullying. A common response was to question the validity of the reports, the line being that 'that sort of thing doesn't happen in this school'.

Although Mike remembered that all the teachers at his primary school tried to stop the bullying, 'especially with the bird incident', his mother described the school's response as generally one of disbelief. It was a case of 'Oh, that child wouldn't do that'. When her son reported incidents to teachers, he was often told: 'Go away, stop whingeing, and get on with it.' This was a response she had not anticipated.

Other parents experienced similar responses. One mother was told by another child that her five-year-old son Hamish (who has learning challenges and some behaviours described as consistent with autism) was being bullied at his first school. When she broached the subject with her son's teacher, she encountered 'a culture of secrecy [in the school]...it doesn't happen here, it won't happen here, it was swept under the carpet'. This was particularly distressing for Hamish's parents, who knew he was unhappy at school. But at that time their questions about what was happening in the playground or in the classroom went unanswered, 'because he didn't have the words to tell us'. Hamish's mother admitted: 'I was so devastated [when I was told he was being bullied] that I didn't really want to know about it...but that just explained so much about Hamish's behaviour.'

Hamish had 'just one friend' at his first school. Now, as an eight-year-old, he talked about how the other children in his new entrant class 'wouldn't let me do my work or draw... wouldn't let me get the felt pens'.

The bullying appeared to be part of a much bigger problem, in that the school seemed unable to provide Hamish with a meaningful education. Hamish's mother recalled:

> They didn't seem to want to do anything with him...he spent the whole day, every day, in the book corner doing nothing...they basically didn't involve him in the curriculum.

Hamish didn't like going to that school because 'the teacher didn't give me good work'. The classroom teacher may have excluded Hamish from the rest of the class by seating him 'at the end [of the classroom]...all by myself'. His parents eventually removed him from the school when the teacher told his mother that Hamish was 'a waste of resources'. They enrolled him in a smaller rural school where he was made welcome: 'He's really happy there, he has lots of friends...and he's getting help [with the curriculum].' Hamish's love of sport was an important basis for developing friendships in his new school, and he had no further experience of bullying.

Seven-year-old Ryan who has epilepsy and co-ordination difficulties, had been physically assaulted by one child at his first primary school, and threatened in the toilets by an older boy who told him he was 'going to kill him'. According to Ryan's mother, the school responded to her report of bullying but the process was not always clear and open:

> I brought it up with the teacher...and it was responded to. The only thing I felt about that school was that whenever you raised anything the alarm bells went off and there was a lot of anxiety. Admittedly they didn't like to hear about [bullying] but I felt that they weren't always very open and straightforward about the whole process of dealing with it there. It was almost like they didn't want to know, because they didn't want to have to face up to the fact that that was happening at their school.

Eight-year-old Tom, who has a physical disability, was also not convinced that the teachers at his school would be able to help him with bullying:

Interviewer: Does anyone try to stop it when this sort of thing happens?
Tom: No.
Interviewer: No, no one ever does?
Tom: And it's girls...don't know why...they just keep doing it.
Interviewer: So what would you like to do to stop it? Do you have any ideas?

Tom:	I would rather have bodyguards [laughs].
Interviewer:	Like the ones in the movies?
Tom:	Yeah.
Interviewer:	So is there anyone you can talk to about being picked on by the bullies?
Tom:	No, not really, can't tell anyone really.
Interviewer:	Yeah? Why is that?
Tom:	I've only got a couple of friends in the school, but they are usually out [playing] with their other friends in the school. But they still talk to me and that.
Interviewer:	Do the teachers ever help you when you are getting bullied?
Tom:	I tell them, but they don't do anything about it really.
Interviewer:	Yeah? What do they say to you when you go and tell them?
Tom:	The only person that really takes care is the principal.
Interviewer:	Yeah? So what does he do?
Tom:	Tells them off…I wish I did have a bodyguard, four bodyguards…they would probably chase after the bullies and say 'Stop it, I'm his bodyguard, keep your hands off him!' [laughs]…
Interviewer:	Have you tried things in the past that have worked or haven't worked to try and stop them?
Tom:	I've tried something that hasn't worked.
Interviewer:	And what was that then?
Tom:	Trying to hold their arms away from me, but they just ripped their hands and arms out. That's the only plan I've had really.

Tom's mother agreed that the teachers were not always helpful, and said she found the school's response to be generally disbelieving: 'Are you sure that it's happening? You're not making it up?' When Tom was asked whether the teachers ever offered him good advice to deal with bullying, he replied: 'No, they just say, "I'll take care of it", and they don't get around to it.' Tom's mother concurred: 'He gets no reaction other than, "Oh, God, you again!" He gets very tearful when that happens.'

The school had tried to protect Tom from bullying by putting him in the school foyer at playtime and lunchtime, but his mother felt that this might be seen as punishing Tom, not the perpetrators. Although the school had a three-step policy to address bullying, it was her impression that the strategy rarely if ever went beyond the first 'talk' stage. She now 'agitated' whenever bullying occurred, and wanted the school to initiate group conferences with the perpetrators, followed by involvement of the parents if bullying continued.

Tom suggested that instead of ignoring him, teachers could help by 'putting bullies in time out, and some kids could say "stop it, that's my friend"; that's all I can think of really'. Despite his unsuccessful attempts to deal with bullying, Tom did have a determined streak: 'I said to one [bully] once, "Do you want my life?" And she said, "Yes". And I said, "Well, you can't have it!"' When we talked with Tom's mother later, she was considering another school for Tom.

Blaming the victim

Some of the children and parents described incidents where behaviour was misinterpreted, and the student with a disability was ultimately blamed for the bullying. When Scott, the secondary student with an autism spectrum disability, was 'lumped together' with another student with an intellectual disability at intermediate, his mother described his reaction:

Mother: Scott's way of reacting to that was to tease the other student...you made a tape.
Scott: Oh yes, I've recorded over it, I've been quite vindictive.
Mother: Scott made a tape up, a song or poem about the student's dog dying and being eaten. The student was very upset about the tape; the teacher found it and that's when you got into trouble.
Scott: Yes.

While Scott was labelled 'the bully' in this instance, his mother suggested that teachers needed to be careful about the way the behaviour of children with disabilities is interpreted. In this and other instances where Scott had shouted and lashed out at students who were annoying him, he had been trying to convey his need for 'space' and to be understood as an individual.

Ryan's mother suggested that what went on in the playground could, at times, be difficult for teachers to interpret accurately, the result being that the victim was sometimes charged with bullying. This was more likely when the student was new to the school, and perhaps the teachers and principal had not yet got to know them:

There was one particular incident where it was all blown up and Ryan was asked to see the principal [because he had hit a girl]...I said [to the principal], 'I can't comment on what happened there, I think if he has hit [her] that's not appropriate, but I would like you to just see if you can ascertain...a little bit more detail about this – what led up to it', given that I had prepared them a lot about how it would be difficult for him entering a new, established group, he was the newcomer and he was very anxious...that he would probably find it difficult socially, and may over-react to any provocation. On that occasion I had some reservations about the way it was dealt with. But since that time, the principal and teachers have made a real effort to get to know and understand Ryan. This has made an enormous difference in terms of his sense of belonging and security at school.

Richard, a ten-year-old with Down Syndrome, was rarely bullied at his primary school. His mother commented:

> Older kids are really good, they really look out for him, it's the younger kids, often six-year-olds and seven-year-olds who are good at setting him up. Once they get to know him, they're fine. It's the wee ones that do it; they repeatedly get in his face to see how he will react and then go running to someone to tell on him.

Like Ryan's mother, she reinforced the importance of teachers looking at the context in which bullying occurred in the playground, so that the child with the disability was not unfairly blamed:

> A kid the other day was lined up with his class walking out and this one kid was going 'pick, pick, pick, pick' [poking] at the other kids as they were walking past. And she poked Richard, and of course Richard went 'Whack!' And a parent saw it. And as the teacher went to say, 'Richard, please don't do that', the parent said, 'It wasn't him first; the girl just poked every child who walked past her'. So it was quite good, but the kids do set him up.

You wouldn't tell Mr Smith...

Some of the children knew that telling certain teachers about bullying was a waste of breath. Eight-year-old Tom, who has a physical disability, believed that the principal was the only person likely to tell the bullies off.

Peter, whose nine-year-old brother has Down Syndrome, also had little faith in the ability of some teachers to deal effectively with bullying:

Interviewer: What do you think would happen if somebody started bullying every day? Do you think the teachers would do anything?
Peter: Probably not, probably not.
Interviewer: Why is that?
Peter: They just tell you to stop, like, they don't really care, telling tales and stuff. They don't really care.
Interviewer: So if you were to tell a teacher that, they'd just say, 'Don't tell tales'?
Peter: Mmmm. Some teachers wouldn't say that, but others don't care. Like if you say someone's beat up someone, they'll say, 'Don't tell tales'.
Interviewer: Even if someone is lying on the ground?
Peter: Yes.

Martin, whose older brother has an autism spectrum disability, distinguished between those teachers who would respond positively and those who would not:

Interviewer: What are the teachers like at helping out?
Martin: Good. My teacher is the strictest teacher in the school.
Interviewer: Does that mean she will do something about it?
Martin: Yeah, if she's on duty.
Interviewer: What sort of things would she do?
Martin: Give them a detention…but some of [the teachers] don't really take any notice of it.
Interviewer: So what do you do then?
Martin: Go to the other duty teacher.
Interviewer: So, you can already tell what a teacher's going to say when you see who it is. You think, oh well, you may as well not bother?

Martin:	Yeah.
Interviewer:	Go and find the other one?
Martin:	Yep, but I never go to Mr Smith, because he's like that.
Interviewer:	So you know that your teacher will do a good job.
Martin:	Yep.

Martin's mother agreed with his perception, and suggested that while all the teachers had been 'great', it was the younger teachers who seemed to know more about creating an inclusive environment in the school: 'The young teachers are not as scared or set in their ideas, I don't know what it is...They're willing to try...'

The teacher's not there...

Ryan's mother also felt that teachers did not always understand the complexity of the context in which bullying occurred, and the challenges faced by children who tried to deal with bullying alone. She was concerned that approaching the teacher for help was not on Ryan's list of priorities. The duty teacher was often inaccessible in the playground, which meant that the problem simply lost its immediacy:

> Ryan wants to try and deal with it himself but he is using some strategies which aren't particularly helpful...what we're trying to do is get him at that point where he's asked [the bullies] to leave him alone, or he's walked off and ignored them and they're pursuing him to hassle him...at that point he goes to the teachers. I don't feel he has a lot of confidence in the teachers in dealing with that...I think one of the problems is that for him – and I can understand it – when it happens there's no one immediately around, so there's a bit of a disincentive to actually go off and find someone.

School contexts that responded positively to reports of bullying

Most of the students in the study were aware that bullying was not acceptable, and that their school did not tolerate it. They knew about the strategies advocated by their school for dealing with bullying, and most felt equipped to use them. In this regard, they were active in confronting bullying. Nonetheless, some of the children described some very subtle and persistent forms of bullying, which even in the most responsive school contexts went unnoticed by teachers. In these situations, the children struggled to respond to bullying in an effective way.

Talk, walk, squawk

In many schools, children are encouraged to use a three-step strategy to deal with bullying: Talk, Walk, Squawk. Ryan had lots of friends, of his own age and older, with whom he played at school and at home. His older friends from his curriculum extension class had become particularly important allies, and supported Ryan when he was teased. They had adapted the Talk, Walk, Squawk strategy and used it on Ryan's behalf:

Interviewer: When you get teased, do your friends ever help you?
Ryan: Yes, they often stick up for me.
Interviewer: That's good. What do they do, Ryan?
Ryan: Well, they do things like, in the first instance... telling them to go away and ignoring them.
Interviewer: Right. Talk, Walk, Squawk, is that right?
Ryan: Well, that's as far as the principal's concerned. But [my friends] would do it differently. Try to scare them off first, then do that bit...They often let me do the final rounds.

Interviewer:	Would they let you have a go first?
Ryan:	No, they would let me have a go last. I leave them to deal with it…Sometimes they hide themselves and then when I couldn't really deal with it, then they'd pop out.
Interviewer:	Do your friends sometimes try and clear it up with the teacher, like if the teacher isn't sure who is doing the teasing?
Ryan:	Well, only my older friends, like twelve, eleven, ten year olds. Not my friends between eight and five.
Interviewer:	The big kids can clear it up for you.
Ryan:	It's actually about 80% big kids…they just go straight to the talk, and they just shortly and calmly talk…and if that doesn't work, they say, 'All right, we're going to tell'.

Scott, the secondary student with an autism spectrum disability, knew that the school took the matter of bullying seriously, and that he could stop the bullying: 'I just ignore it, or if it is of sufficient magnitude, I report it.' He admitted, however, that while teachers usually responded quite 'intensely' to reports of bullying, 'sometimes it takes a long time for them to react, teachers have a lot to do'. The best way for students to respond was by 'ignoring it, reporting it, avoiding where [the bullies] probably are', and for bullies to 'find other ways to release any potential aggression', while teachers should 'punish the bullies'. But also:

> …bullies should realise what the effect is that they are having on the other individual and hopefully you know that someone actually examines what is going on for the bully as well.

An immediate response: 'If there is an issue, it's bam!'

Some schools acted to stamp out bullying by responding to incidents immediately. Bullying was rarely an issue at Hamish's new school, according to his parents, because if anything happened in the playground:

> ...the principal got up in assembly and told the children what she had heard happened. She'd either spoken to the children involved...or was going to speak to them...she would explain to the whole community why a child was different...she would explain why and it's like children had this understanding of why so-and-so acted in such-and-such a way and she would go on and on. You wouldn't call it a lecture – it was more like a lesson...and I used to think, okay you can stop now, but she would just keep on going, and you could see those children would think about it and if ever there was an issue, it was bam! Just like that. There was the most amazing community spirit in the school [when she was principal].

Leah's mother commented that in her daughter's small rural primary school, 'bullying was not an issue, because the culture of the school was such that "the kids wouldn't think to do it"'. At intermediate school, however, when her mother heard that Leah was being encouraged to use her white cane to chase other children, she went straight to the teacher:

> The kids in her class were talked to about it and I've heard no more about it...The teacher said yes, it would certainly be addressed [as] it is inappropriate. So he was totally supportive...we have a very good, open relationship with clear communication both ways.

Personalised strategies to deal with bullying

Some of the students had developed their own strategies and had become relatively independent and effective in responding to bullying. While some teachers might not consider these strategies to be the most desirable, the students used their own understanding of the realities of bullying, the culture of the student group, and the likely response of teachers to come up with their own unique solutions. The experiences of these students suggest that a school's anti-bullying procedures may need to reflect more accurately the realities of playground life.

'Kick back, kick butt'

Mike, the older student with a physical disability had felt 'pissed' by the bullying that occurred at primary school; but as a fourteen-year-old at secondary school he had gained some independent strategies for dealing with bullying:

> If I get bullied, I pull the finger and say 'Piss off' to them...that's the best solution for me, go 'Piss off' and some other kinds of words...just give [it] back...Kick back, kick butt.

The effect of this strategy at secondary school was to reduce the perceived impact of bullying: 'They got pissed and did it more, I did it more and they got pissed, and then they didn't do it any more...something inside of me just told me to kick back.'

Avoidance and confrontation

Scott's mother described the avoidance strategy her son had adopted at secondary school:

> Scott has learned to cope with bullying himself. He will stay to the end, be the last somewhere, sit by himself,

avoiding, keeping himself safe. One of his teachers made the comment that Scott knows how to keep himself safe.

In other situations Scott had been more assertive in his response to teasing. His mother commented that he'd reacted in quite an intelligent way:

> ...he's been called all sorts of horrible things in the past, like 'mental', and the usual sorts of things that people call kids that are a bit different. But he was called 'schizophrenic' once...obviously this person didn't know what schizophrenia was, and Scott did. Scott said to the person, 'Do I look like somebody who can hear voices in my head?', and the person sort of was taken aback because in fact he didn't know what he was talking about.

Scott's family and a psychologist who supported him had also helped him to develop new ways of dealing with bullying at school:

> Scott has learnt to come out with comments...we try and come up with things for him to say...the psychologist has also helped him to role play these situations too, just to laugh and throw it back, and just don't let those things upset you.

'Shoo them off'

Eight-year-old Ryan preferred to deal with bullying himself, relying on his friends as backup support only if necessary. He had adapted the school's anti-bullying strategy to suit his own style, and to meet the complex demands of the playground environment: 'I scare them off. I growl at them. I pretend to throw a fireball at them and that scares them off because they think I'm a warrior'. These strategies were not always effective, however: 'If they don't go away then they call me a copy-cat and call me dumb.'

Ryan's mother understood why he wanted to take control of the situation:
> ...he feels he really needs to assert himself a lot, like he's intimidated by these girls, so he feels he has to say things in a big loud voice to frighten them away...He wants to shoo them away really [but] I don't think they're particularly receptive.

While Ryan knew about the school's bullying procedures, he identified some shortcomings when it came to putting the procedures into practice in the playground:

Interviewer: Do you do anything else to stop them [bullying you]?

Ryan: Well, our principal says that you talk, you talk to them, then you walk away from the person, [then you] squawk – tell the teacher. But if the person [who bullied you] *knows* you are telling the teacher...well, I usually tell them, 'I'm going to see the teacher about you', and then they try to run away. So I *don't* tell them...Otherwise, they will get to the teacher first and trick the teacher into telling on [blaming] me.

Ryan had devised a complex strategy involving shortcuts. This meant getting to the duty teacher first, with support from friends to ensure that the truth about who had really done the bullying was revealed, and that he was not blamed:

Ryan: I always take the shortcuts to the teacher and I never tell [the bullies] I use the shortcut. The shortcut is through the adventure playground and they never use that way, because more people walk through the main course...that way I get to the duty teacher first...and then when I see [the bullies] before they see me I tell the teacher. I don't want them to know. And before they see

	me, when they're about 100 metres away, then I say [to the teacher] 'there's that person, there's the person', and I point to them...I need to run [then] so they won't see me, and usually I run in beneath a crowd of people...the teacher then tells them [off] because I told her, but if I stay then the kid might know I told the teacher. That's why I never stay.
Interviewer:	So you don't stay because if you did stay –
Ryan:	The kid would trick the teacher and say it was my fault.

Ryan's mother and his teacher were working together to help Ryan find effective ways to respond to bullying. She felt very well supported in this, although she worried that 'it's sometimes quite hard to arrange a meeting...we're waiting to establish a time'.

Discussion

What are the children telling us about bullying?

The fact that nine of the eleven students with disabilities in our study described incidents of bullying suggests that children with disabilities may be at least as likely as their non-disabled peers (and possibly more likely) to be bullied. This is consistent with suggestions made by other writers (Sullivan, 2000; Evans et al., 1992; Mooney and Smith, 1995). For those nine students in our study, bullying was or had been a persistent, ongoing issue. However, the range of experiences and the different histories revealed by the individual students and their families show the uniqueness of their situations. At the same time, there are patterns emerging. This book is not an attempt at a definitive explanation but a description of those patterns.

The bullying reported by the children was often personal, and involved other students picking on their perceived weaknesses. Ryan's mother talked about children 'picking on his little vulnerabilities', and Tom felt he was bullied because 'I'm a disability'. Bullying included direct physical and emotional attacks, and apparently deliberate isolation.

The experiences of students in our study also raise questions about some of the assumptions about bullies and defenders in the current literature (see, for example, Sullivan, 2000). The literature suggests that boys might bully more than girls; but in our study girls were often actively involved in bullying, particularly in the teasing of boys with disabilities at primary school. Also, while girls are recognised as likely defenders of bullying victims, the boys in our study found support in their male friends. The children and their parents indicated that bullying by girls may occur out of the sight of teachers (which is reminiscent of Sullivan's notion of girls as 'hidden bullies'), and that teachers may not always understand the wider context in which bullying has occurred. Ryan's mother, for example, suggested that Ryan lost confidence in and was cynical about teachers' responses, which were based on the inaccurate assumption that 'the boys are the baddies and the girls are the goodies'. This meant that in some cases the child with the disability was blamed, rather than the perpetrator; the bullying was ignored by teachers; or children with disabilities (and in some cases their friends) were left to deal with the situation in their own way. For schools, the more physical forms of bullying may be more obvious than the verbal forms, and therefore easier to respond to.

The features identified and described in this chapter reflect what was happening for these students as they saw it. The study focused on children's actual experiences of bullying at school as 'an inherently social practice, one that happens *between* people' (Maharaj et al., 2000, p.19). It also acknowledged the much broader social categorisation between 'disabled' and 'non-disabled' as possibly *underlying* these social processes. Is bullying due to the 'disability' as perceived by other children? A common feature that describes relations between students is seeing the other person as 'different', as 'the other', which leads to isolation and exclusion (Purdue et al., 2001). In this case, disability alerts some children to the idea that this person is 'not like me'. Tom did feel that other children bullied him 'because I'm a disability', and Scott understood that bullying originated in a 'lack of tolerance'.

But this simplistic dichotomy was not seen as the only reason for being isolated, and other bases for differentiation were also suggested. Tom noted that it was not just his disability that separated him out; it was also the fact that he was not part of the 'kids in big gangs'. Disability does not need to be the basis for differentiation, either; as Martin pointed out, his brother AJ created attachment through his humour, which provided a means of overcoming or challenging the isolation that may be associated with a 'disability' label. Similarly, Hamish had a lot of friends in his small rural school with whom he shared an interest in sport.

Labelling 'the other' as different may also occur *among* disabled students. Aidan's mother attributed his being bullied to an identified difference between the students with learning and behaviour problems and Aidan who has an intellectual disability. Aidan's sister also indicated a willingness to challenge the bullying by reconnecting him and sending him 'on his way with a friend'. She indicated that other mainstream students did show concern and care for Aidan, suggesting that there may be an understanding in this school of 'sameness' and belonging in relation to students with disabilities (Maeroff, 1998; Purdue et al., 2001). There were also indications that where relationships were not established in the past, for example at primary school, students may be more likely to focus on difference by emphasising the disability, rather than accepting the student with the disability as they would any other student.

The isolation of some students may have been maintained by name-calling, which served to reinforce ideas about difference. Scott's lack of friends led to other students teasing him about being alone, and the name-calling would occur only when he was isolated. Ryan was also picked on because of his 'little vulnerabilities', but although some children attempted to emphasise his 'difference', he also received support from other students and teachers who knew him well. Bullying for Ryan, then, did not lead to isolation. This relationship between friendship and bullying is explored further in Chapter 3.

Are schools part of the problem or part of the solution?

Some schools were understood to be inherently safe places where bullying rarely if ever occurred. Small rural schools in particular had an inclusive community focus, and 'the kids wouldn't think to bully'. Children we spoke to from these schools knew what bullying was, but had never seen examples in their own school. If any incidents of bullying arose, they were noted and attended to immediately as a whole-school issue.

These small rural schools may be understood to have a culture that welcomes, supports and nurtures diverse needs.

Students are accepted as they are, and are not expected to struggle to be 'normal' (Corbett, 1999). Schools that value diversity reflect this ethos through the actions of their principals, teachers and others. Bullying rarely occurs, and when it does it is dealt with immediately. In these schools there is an emphasis on 'humanness' and on children with disabilities being 'like us' (Bogdan and Taylor, 1992).

Corbett (1999) and others (see, for example, Brantlinger, 1997; Oliver, 1992) suggest that creating an inclusive ethos is about values. The now outdated concept of *integration* emphasised the responsibility of people with disabilities and their families (as well as other individuals defined and marginalised by the majority as 'different') to make the effort to integrate themselves into the mainstream culture. Hence schools were not required to change. *Inclusion*, on the other hand, places the onus on the school to respond to diversity in its students by creating a climate of receptiveness, flexibility and sensitivity. While integration is about *individuals*; inclusion is about *community values*.

Some of the schools described by participants in our study may have contributed to bullying by maintaining a school culture in which disability is associated with deviance and difference. Skrtic (1995) suggests that the field of 'special' education locates disability within assumptions of pathology and normative differences, so that to label a child as 'special' or as having 'special needs' may also result in the child being labelled as 'different'. Within this context, children with disabilities may then experience 'exclusion' (Purdue et al., 2001; Purdue et al., 1998). The actions of some teachers described in our study may be seen as also reinforcing the idea of 'disability as difference'. When Hamish began school as a new entrant, he was placed 'at the end [of the classroom]... by myself', and little effort was made to include him in the curriculum or the activities of the school.

For other students with disabilities, teachers failed to recognise that their experience of bullying may be different from that of other children. Teachers may need to respond to bullying in ways that are sensitive to the individual child and to the context in which the bullying takes place. Several students with disabilities reported that teachers did not always believe them or deal with the bullying when they reported it. When Mike was bullied he was told to 'stop whingeing', and Tom's mother described the reaction of teachers as one of 'Oh God, not you again'. Some students were cynical about teachers' ability to respond to bullying in supportive and productive ways, and distinguished between teachers who would help and those who were never likely to.

Some parents also felt that difficulties arose when teachers did not know their children well. The mothers of Ryan and Scott felt that their children's behaviour had been misinterpreted as bullying when it had in fact been a response to bullying. In these situations, there was a risk that the victim would be blamed rather than supported. Ryan's mother stressed that teachers needed to take time to talk with parents, to share information and to solve problems.

For schools or teachers to deny that bullying is occurring would seem to be a denial that power is part of the social relations between students in schools. Indeed, it may be easier to 'not see' the bullying if the student does not have the ability to communicate to others that it is occurring. Teachers may also fail to examine the specific context in which an incident occurs, leading to a blaming of the victim.

We did not find that the children in our study were more at risk of *being* a bully, as suggested by Whitney et al., 1994 (cited in Sullivan, 2000). However, the message from some of the parents was that their children's behaviour may be misinterpreted as bullying. While they did not approve of their sons hitting or lashing out at others, some parents pleaded with teachers to get to know their children in order to understand their behaviour better. Scott's mother described his loud and lashing out behaviour as an indication that he needed space. Ryan's mother explained to his principal and teacher that he would feel anxious when he started school, and that he sometimes dealt with difficult situations in ways that teachers and students might not understand at first.

These experiences suggest that teachers' knowledge of their students is critical, and that teachers need to take time to talk with parents about their child and about the wider school context, particularly when the child is new to the school. Ryan's mother felt it was important to spend time preparing the principal, teachers and students in the school, so that they would understand Ryan, his disability, and the way he behaved. His mother continued to address issues relating to bullying and relationships as they arose at school, but was aware that finding the time to meet with teachers was not always easy.

The students themselves often had very clear expectations, based on their experiences, of how individual teachers would respond to reports of bullying. These expectations strongly influenced their decisions about whether to 'squawk' and who to 'squawk' to. Strategies such as 'Talk, Walk, Squawk' may offer students a way of dealing with a bullying problem as it happens, but the effectiveness of the strategy will depend on what the consequences of 'squawking' are, should the child get to that point. Teachers need to appreciate that children with disabilities may experience frequent and persistent bullying, and may therefore report it frequently. If a child 'squawks' often, teachers should be alerted to the fact that there is a real problem, rather than ignoring it or accusing the child of whingeing.

Children with disabilities have to overcome a number of disadvantages in their lives, both at school and in their wider communities. The parents and children in our study identified some of the features of a school culture and context in which bullying is allowed to survive. Others described school contexts in which bullying is unheard of, where children with disabilities are welcomed and valued. One parent commented:

> [In the first school] it was just denial, 'we never see bullying going on here, we would know if anything is going on'. But at the new school, you can see a totally different picture…We were just blown away. It was like, wow! This is an open policy school. You can discuss anything and everything, whereas over there, at the other school, you'd be shivering in your boots if you had to go and ask the teacher. It's just the most wonderfully welcoming and warm place.

Schools have a responsibility to ensure that all children, including those with disabilities, can grow, learn and develop in a safe and socially supportive environment.

CHAPTER 3
Students' Friendships and Relationships

'I'm looking for a new friend... I'm trying and trying and trying to look for a friend, but I just don't know any of their names...' (Leah, aged 11)

While the siblings we interviewed talked freely about the friends they played with at school and at home, the students with disabilities described relationships with other children that covered a wide range. Three of the students described close friendships which had developed at school and now extended beyond the school gates to their homes. But this was not the typical picture for the other seven students with disabilities. They experienced a range of relationships, characterised by a lack of close friendships. We have categorised those relationships as follows:
'I have no friends.'
'My friends also have disabilities'
'My friends are younger or they are girls' [in the case of boys with disabilities]
'I'm popular, but I don't have real friends (my friends are my sibling's friends)'
'I have "sometimes" friends'
'I have "real" friends'

The students with disabilities rarely described themselves as lonely or as lacking in friends. They usually described their relationships with other children in terms of their day-to-day experiences at school. Parents, on the other hand, were more likely to take a critical perspective on their children's relationships with others, often identifying their children as lonely and as having no 'real' or 'close' friends.

'I have no friends'

Scott, a fifteen-year-old with an autism spectrum disability, had no friends at school. He 'hated' break times, and spent much of his time alone. People with autism can have major difficulties with the social conventions that most of us learn readily and apply without difficulty. Social rules and conventions, such as how and when to look at others, how long to wait when responding to a question, making eye contact, and using appropriate language in different contexts, can present endless challenges (Watson et al. 1999). Scott's mother recognised the barriers that his disability imposed to the development of friendship. She described the real challenges faced by both parents and teachers in trying to overcome those barriers:

> It's just that I don't have any ideas how to solve any of the social [problems] – the lack of social contact he has. His recreation and social time – he's at a loss. It's really hard to solve the problem for him! Because he can't! That's the nature of his disorder…he's on his own. He always walks around on his own at school, but he doesn't make it easy! I've seen other kids speak to him and say, 'Hi, Scott!', and he sort of goes 'Ummm…', like this. It's taken a long time to teach him to say hello back to people and now when he does he mutters it down in his boots. He actually excludes himself, which is hard.

Although he now recognised that he did in fact want friends, Scott felt that he had more in common with his teachers than his fellow students. His intense interest in the hard sciences, for example, was not shared by his peer group:

Scott:	I would like to have some friends but I just, it's just I don't really have any and, well, things don't seem to be changing.
Interviewer:	Has it always been that way for you?
Scott:	Yes, but [it's] only recently that I've actually wanted friends...I've developed socially quite a bit.
Interviewer:	Oh, so you're ready to develop some friendships?
Scott:	Yes, just now it seems too late, well it's starting to get that way, it's not as easy as it would have been in the past...I like how I can sort of talk to teachers on a, well, human level. I mean, it's not like they're just old people who live at the school and come out of cupboards, you can actually talk to them as people...I like to talk to my group teacher who taught last year's physics and I'm extremely interested in physics...and in pure mathematics, chemistry and various other sciences...I share a lot of interests with them and talk about those things...I've discovered that some teachers don't know what I'm talking about. Even if they do specialise around that subject...I don't think I have shared ideals [with other students], like there's no one in the school that enjoys reading quantum physics books. I guess when I get home I stay in my bedroom for two hours reading quantum physics constantly, writing down notes, formulas, equations...
Interviewer:	Yes, it's hard finding somebody who's interested in the things you're interested in.
Scott:	Like there aren't many that even know what the natural logarithm is.

Scott's teacher aide and teachers at secondary school were aware of his isolation from other students and were developing strategies to encourage him to be part of the student group. But his mother remained concerned about what happened during break times:

> The teacher aide has tried to just encourage Scott to be part of the group – mainly in school time though, it's not out-of-class time. Using that formal structured time when they have to move into small groups, because otherwise he would exclude himself and he would always be the last part of the group because he would stand back...the teacher aide would make sure Scott was in early. Even teachers in their way have included him in groups so he wasn't the only one who was left last. Just very subtle things like that, but that's mainly in class time. I think it's more problematic in the play area – in the unstructured lunch hours. I don't know if any teaching role has ever been played but then I guess that's their time out too.

Isolation from their peers had been an issue for both Hamish (now aged eight) and AJ (now aged twelve) at their first primary schools. Both children had experienced exclusion by teachers and peers, and had since moved on to other primary schools which their parents described as welcoming and supportive. They agreed that the teaching practices adopted in their sons' first schools contributed to their physical and social exclusion from the peer group. Hamish was essentially uninvolved in the curriculum:

> [The teacher] didn't seem to want to do anything with him...he spent the whole day, every day, in the book corner doing nothing...We were told by the teacher that he was 'a waste of resources'.

Hamish was unhappy at school, and according to his mother

had just one friend there. In the classroom he was physically isolated from the other children by having his desk located 'at the end [of the classroom]…all by myself'. Now attending a smaller rural school, Hamish was 'really happy…he has lots of friends…and he's getting help [with the curriculum]'. In contrast to his previous school, he was now sitting in the centre of the classroom, an integral part of classroom life.

AJ had a similar history. His mother described his first school experience as a 'nightmare' with lasting repercussions:

> We thought we'd chosen the right school, and did all the right things for the transition…they just didn't want him there and made it very difficult and were just baby-sitting him really. Plonked at the back of the room with his headphones on listening to music and [told to] go and play outside with a ball and that was it. He used to play up, he knew he wasn't doing the same as the other kids so he would play up. And they couldn't see that of course. It was a nightmare when I look back, it was just dreadful. They wouldn't let him stay till 3 pm, he had to go home at 2 and I had to take him home at lunchtimes. [For] swimming I had to go with him and I was seven months pregnant. It was just a nightmare. The final straw was when the whole school went to the Blind Foundation to sing to the blind people…AJ had to stay at school and he was just desperately upset because he wanted to go with all the other kids and sing…How hypocritical could they be? They were going to sing to the blind people but they couldn't take their own disabled kiddie with them.

AJ's mother complained to the principal, who seemed unable to understand that AJ 'had feelings like anyone else':

> The principal just couldn't understand that AJ was upset because he didn't go with the kids and that I was upset because of that…so we of course had a big to-do. We went

to the Ministry of Education, the Board of Trustees was called in...we knew we could force them to go by the rules, to have him at school until 3 pm and so on, but what was the point because we couldn't change their attitude...the school didn't want to make it work. All the offers I'd given them, all the information I had given them, everything I had given them, they didn't want to know. What's the point? We moved schools.

According to AJ's mother, the 'exclusive' attitude and actions of the teacher and principal contributed to AJ's overall experience of social isolation at the school:

Because they treated him differently, the kids did as well. He wasn't allowed to be there at lunchtime so he only had playtime in the morning to play with the kids, so he couldn't form any friendships. He wasn't included in the classroom activities so he wasn't part of the classroom so the kids excluded him in the playground as well.

In sharp contrast, AJ's new school expected him to be like the other kids:

...so he is, he is just like the other kids. He is included in everything and the kids in the playground include him in things and look out for him. Just being one of the kids at school.

'My friends also have disabilities'

Leah's mother shared these concerns about friendship for her twelve-year-old daughter. Leah's disability, like Scott's, created barriers to the formation of friendships. Her low vision and limited spatial awareness made it difficult for her to pick up on the subtle visual cues that friendship development often relies on, such as body language and turn-taking. Leah also pointed out that it is difficult for her to 'find' other students in the playground, and to learn the names of other students who might be potential friends.

Leah's mother was aware that she had no friends at intermediate school, other than a tenuous relationship with two girls who also had disabilities:

> She has no real friends. It's very hard for her. One of the reasons I wanted her there [at intermediate school] was to be with her peers from primary school, so she wouldn't drop into this black hole...but only two moved to the same intermediate. She is quite lonely. For a start she was eating lunch on her own...She would say, 'I have to walk into school on my own, Mum, like a lot of other kids meet at the gate and walk in together'. Leah didn't have that.

Even at primary school, Leah did not have close friends. She spent much of her free time playing with younger new entrant children, 'where she was accepted and tolerated and was at their level'. Leah's mother commented that if she was asked about who her friends were, she would say 'I don't know', or she would nominate 'somebody she sat with at lunch... they're all her friends'.

The student most likely to seek Leah out at intermediate school was a student who had behavioural disabilities. This student seemed to have a limited understanding of the boundaries established in the school, and Leah was aware of this:

Leah: [At playtime and lunchtime] I sometimes walk around with Maria and Kate, but Kate always annoys me.

Interviewer: What does she do to annoy you?

Leah: The first time she took me outside the back grounds [an area designated out of bounds]. And [sigh] Kate is not a very good girl...

Interviewer: Mmmm, is she your friend?

Leah:	Yeah.
Interviewer:	Do you play with her at lunchtime as well?
Leah:	Yeah, but sometimes I can't find her.
Interviewer:	What happens if you can't find her?
Leah:	I just walk around by myself.
Interviewer:	Mmmm, and what's that like?
Leah:	Not good.

For Leah's mother, the fact that Kate had taken Leah outside the school grounds was 'a huge safety issue, but Leah just says, "I've got to do it", so now we just have to teach her that it's okay to say no'.

Leah was unhappy that she did not have friends to spend time with at playtime and lunchtime, but she had few strategies for dealing with this problem. She had apparently discarded the idea that her own classmates might be her friends, and was anxious to seek out new friendships with children from other classes. But after seven months in the school, she did not know these other children and nor did she know *how* to get to know them: 'I'm looking for a new friend...I'm trying and trying and trying to look for a friend, but I just don't know any of their names...'

At Leah's Individual Education Plan (IEP) meeting, her mother emphasised the importance of friendships and relationships as part of the planning context for her daughter: 'One of the first niggles I had with the teacher was, "How can we encourage this, put in some strategies?"' In response to Leah's comment about arriving at school in the morning, she and the teacher worked out a roster system for other students in the class to meet Leah at the gate:

> ...it was a bit artificial and I'm a bit philosophically challenged by it...but it has worked...recently her teacher said the kids run up to check the roster in the morning, so

hopefully that formal bit will be taken away, so it was just getting them to say, 'Hey, it's OK to be walking with Leah'.

The teacher also set up a buddy system in the hope that this might generate friendships within her own class, and talked with the class about supporting each other. But Leah's mother wrestled with the idea that friendships cannot be forced:

> I think at the level we are at now at intermediate – the teacher has spent a bit of time talking about these sorts of issues, but you've got to understand that twelve-year-olds, they want to do their own thing. They don't want hangers-on.

This issue, which according to Leah's mother was 'the hardest thing', remained unresolved for this family.

Aidan was the only student in the study who was not taught in a regular classroom. He attended a Special Unit at his high school, and his friends were also students with disabilities who attended the unit. Aidan's mother described his friendships as fragile: 'It's Campbell at the moment, but then next week…you know.' Much of his out-of-school time was spent with his older sister Kristin and her friends, who had 'always known Aidan'. He also had a younger friend with whom he shared a hobby, and the two occasionally spent some time together at weekends. Kristin confirmed that while older students at the school (particularly seventh-formers) would 'keep an eye on Aidan', it was the other students from the unit that he spent his break times with:

> I see Aidan pushing Mike around in his wheelchair, quite often, and there's Campbell, and there's another boy in a wheelchair as well, same sort of thing. Sophie, Aidan and Campbell I see quite often are pushing them around.

Aidan's mother felt that secondary schools were difficult places to establish friendships because of the movement between classes:

High schools are different from primary and intermediate schools because you don't have your own class, they go from class to class with their different [subjects]…that's how I thought the Special Unit might be more stable, it's a classroom, whereas if he were fully mainstreamed there's no set classroom so I thought it would be quite confusing for him, especially if he didn't have support in every classroom…It'd be fine if he had a full-time teacher aide but the world's not like that, I'm afraid.

'My friends are younger or they are girls'

Some of the students with disabilities spent their recreation time at school playing with younger children. Some boys with disabilities played primarily with girls, unlike their age peers who preferred same-sex friendships. Richard and Andrew also spent much of their break time at primary school with their teacher aide.

Leah's sister Anna said that at the age of eleven Leah either played with the new entrants at her primary school or spent time alone. Similarly Peter described his brother Richard, a ten-year-old with Down Syndrome, as:

…just walking around the playground with his teacher aide [at playtime], and he plays with other little children that are playing with cars and things like that. He plays with Petra in the sandpit…his friends are girls, my friends are boys.

Richard shared a teacher aide with two younger children who also had disabilities, so the three children often joined up at playtime and lunchtime. Richard's mother commented:

He finds [friendships] really hard because he doesn't have the appropriate [skills] – well, ten-year-old boys are so far in advance of him physically and the games they play he's not interested in, playing a ball game or things they get up to. Ten-year-old boys are really a lot more advanced in their play skills and things. He gets on with the girls, they'll mother him and smother him...there are two little girls in his class who love him to death. He's been to their birthday parties and they've been to his. These are the only two kids whose birthday parties he's been to.

Ben, a six-year-old with a learning and behavioural disability, was in his second year at primary school. At playtime and lunchtime he mostly played with new entrant children, or stood on the periphery of games played by older children. Ben's sister Hayley thought that Ben 'played by himself with hula hoops or skipping ropes'. When asked what made her think this, she said that Ben was 'sometimes a bit serious when he comes home'. When Ben was asked who he played with at school, he named two new entrant children (a girl and a boy) who had just started school, and described playing imaginary games with them. He could not name any other friends who might be 'just friends' rather than 'best friends'.

According to Ben's mother, he had no close friends: 'I don't think there is anyone.' This perception was confirmed when Ben decided to invite to his sixth birthday party two boys from his rugby team; a friend from his preschool days; 'and just Mark from his classroom'. She was not aware that Mark was a particular friend with whom Ben spent time at school:

I usually try to avoid the junior playground. I've got to walk past it, but quite often you find he's with the older boys but they're there and he's just that little bit back from the rest of the group. He's not quite fully included...I think it's a pity for him.

Ben's mother was generally unsure about his social experiences at school, and his teachers appeared to convey little information about this aspect of his school life. Ben's behaviour meant that other children might perceive him 'as the bully', and his mother worried that 'perhaps they just don't want to play with him'. While the other children at school were 'very quick to go and tell the teacher if Ben does anything', he too had been on the receiving end of bullying:

> He came home very upset and it took me three or four days to get it out of him that the kids were calling him 'fatty'. He didn't want to go back to school and I said that to the teacher and within a couple of days apparently it had all stopped and we've never heard about it since…I tried to make it into a positive thing by saying that if he's going to be an All Black he needs to be big…and he was, 'OK, cool!' So it really wasn't a problem after that.

While Ben's mother acknowledged that he 'could be a bully', she wondered if his disability set him up for other children to see him as a problem:

> With the other kids [who hassle them] the children at school might not report to teachers so often, but with Ben they seem to be in there telling the teacher [every time]. I'd say it happens daily and that can't be good for him.

Ben's mother was not sure if his teachers were aware of his lack of friends at school. Like other parents in the study, she was concerned that some of the teaching strategies used with Ben could contribute to his isolation:

> When a different teacher is in charge, Ben is removed from the classroom…At one stage last term…he was obviously disruptive so he was sat at a desk all by himself…which to me meant he was isolated…a student teacher was running the classroom for part of the morning and Ben was taken down to another room while the teachers had a meeting, [and] they let him play on the floor in there. He's going to

expect that to happen all the time and once again...he's being isolated...It's definitely telling the other kids that Ben is different and I think it's telling him that he's different...To me it's not giving him the chance to be with another teacher. He's being removed because they expect him to play up.

'I'm popular, but I don't have real friends (my friends are my sibling's friends)'

Twelve-year-old AJ was popular with the other children at his primary school, and they were friendly towards him. But his mother conceded that:

> I couldn't say he's got friends...the kids are really good with him. There's two or three boys in the class who really look out for him and the girls of course do that too which is nice. He's never had friends come round, and he's never been invited to birthday parties...I really feel for him but he doesn't seem to be particularly worried. But he loves it when his brother and sister have friends around to play, and he wants to go to their friends' places to play too. So, he's sort of realising that's what you do, but he doesn't seem to mind, I don't know, he just doesn't seem to be aware that he hasn't got friends. It's hard, especially when they do topics on friends in class. He doesn't seem to be aware of it, so it's silly me worrying, but you do, your heart goes out to them. Missing out on things.

AJ's school included and taught a diverse group of children, and was 'very accepting'. AJ was 'just another kid...he doesn't stick out like a sore toe'. His mother stressed, however, that AJ's approach to play was different from that of his peers, and that his peers had recognised and adapted to it:

> ...he doesn't play with other kids, he'll play alongside. He loves watching kids play but he prefers to stand back and

watch rather than join in...He'd like to join in with them [at times]. Like if he wanted to have a go at soccer the kids will let him have a kick, he doesn't need to play a whole soccer game. He just wants to get a kick and he's quite happy, and the kids let him do that. They're really good.

Andrew, a nine-year-old with Down Syndrome attended his local primary school with a younger sibling. His father described his relationships with other children at school as very positive and supportive:

Really good. When he had his birthday, he would invite everyone in his class, you know? He does [talk about some children more often]. Yeah. He will say, like, Jacob, and there was another boy who left school last year. Our [other] children have friends coming around home.

Andrew enjoyed playing with his brother's friends, but did not often have his own peers home to play. He enjoyed playing on the Playstation, and his mother saw this as providing an important context for learning social skills such as taking turns and teaching others how to play. He had just recently visited a school friend's home for the first time, and according to his father was 'really happy about that'. As with AJ, Andrew's outgoing personality and soccer skills were considered assets when it came to relationships at school and at home:

The other kids are really good to him. I think one of the things is his character, he makes teachers laugh...Yeah, he's likeable, and I think this makes people want to come to this house...most of the time at school he plays with other kids. He is really good at soccer because his teacher aide last year was really good at soccer, he could go around and behind dribbling the ball. He has definitely developed a skill from soccer.

'I have "sometimes" friends'

Eight-year-old Tom was bullied at his primary school, particularly by girls, and felt powerless to do anything to stop it. His physical disability made it difficult to keep up with his more energetic peers, and he had few if any friends to call on for support: 'The kids in my class don't really play with me.' At playtime and lunchtime he just 'walked around', mostly on his own. When asked what he would prefer to do at playtime and lunchtime, he replied: 'Play with my friends.' In fact Tom had no friends in his own class, and identified two older boys for whom he was a 'backup' friend: '[At lunchtime] they're just with their other friends, because sometimes their friends just back off them...and I'm there to play with them, to back up. [I'm] the backup.'

Tom realised that friends could help to protect him from frequent bullying at school, but his 'backup' friends were generally unavailable, and he spent much of his recreation time alone:

Interviewer:	So is there anyone you can talk to about being picked on by the bullies?
Tom:	No, not really, can't tell anyone really.
Interviewer:	Yeah? Why's that?
Tom:	I've only got a couple of friends in the school, but they are usually out [playing] with their other friends in the school. But they still talk to me and that.

Ironically, one of the school's solutions to Tom being bullied was to place him in the foyer away from the bullies, which could be seen as contributing to his isolation. Tom's mother named three children he played with at school, but she described these friendships as 'on again, off again' because his physical disability meant he was unable to keep up with them. His friendships tended to be school-based, and focused on shared activities, particularly playing on the computer. After-school arrangements with friends were difficult, because Tom's friends either lived too far away or were involved in other activities. Tom's mother also found it difficult to support after-school visits because 'life is just too busy'.

Ten-year-old Richard's friendships were mostly with girls, and were described by his mother as 'superficial':

> The three children he has most to do with were in his class last year and he will be in with them again next year. I mean, they're superficial friendships, but they're friendships. Those wee girls stand by him all the time…they mother him, they smother him, but they're all just around the same age as him, a wee bit younger, but they make sure he's organised [in class].

During break times, however, Richard spent much of his time alone, but was nonetheless happy:

> He doesn't really play. He's a solitary player, he still kind of likes to do what he wants to do. He doesn't really care if no one else wants to do it too, he's quite happy.

Opportunities to develop relationships with other children outside school were limited by his challenging social behaviours:

> He tends to blast his way through everything…so he doesn't get a lot of chances any more…he can act completely anti-socially…his cousin and an older sixth-former look after him on Saturday morning which he loves.

It was also difficult for Richard's mother to support out-of-school friendships because both she and his father worked.

'I have "real" friends'

Three of the students with disabilities (Hamish, aged eight; Ryan, aged seven; and Mike, aged thirteen) described friendships that developed at school and now extended beyond the school gates to home. These relationships seemed similar to the close friendships described by their siblings, and often developed around shared interests, particularly sports. The students talked about their friends by name, and referred to their 'best friends'.

Hamish named five boys as his best friends, and three girls and one boy as his best friends in his class at his small rural school. (This was in contrast to his first school, where he had just one friend.) His friends were similar in age, except for one older friend who also had a disability. At lunchtime Hamish liked to 'play with my friends' – rugby in winter, and scrag and cricket in summer. He played sport on Saturdays in a club team that included some of his school friends. According to his parents, his love of sports and the size of the school made it easy for him to make friends:

> It's just part of his life, being with friends…it's a little school, the kids are all playing together and you have experience of all ages…sports are very important in terms of friends. Something that they can all get together around. It's a common shared activity.

Hamish's mother described him as:

> …very sociable, and when he's being sociable, which is most of the time, it's great. But small incidents which would not upset a normal person just blow up in Hamish's face. If something goes wrong, he wouldn't respond to the child, he'd come to us.

Hamish's parents had encouraged him to approach a teacher for assistance if challenging social situations arose at school:
> So we've always told him, 'Please go and get an adult, get a big person', and he often tells me stories about how he's gone and got somebody because so-and-so did something, which makes him sound like a little tell-tale but these days that sort of stuff is brought out in the open and he never gets told off for it.

Hamish's parents supported his friendships through social events with other families, and by having his friends home to play. Hamish also played at his friends' homes. His parents did not see the teachers as having a particular role to play in supporting friendships: 'It's a small school and because they play rugby in the winter and cricket in the summer, it all just happened.' They did note, however, that the teachers would join in when the children played sport and that this could have an important moderating effect on Hamish's relationships with other children:
> The teacher gets in there and plays with them. And that's the interesting part. When they're playing and there's no teacher there Hamish can get himself into some fairly heavy scraps because he likes to, well, he has his own interpretation of the rules. But when there's a teacher there, an adult to be a moderator, they're wonderful. The kids need the teacher for Hamish.

The school also had 'the most amazing community spirit…it's just the most wonderfully welcoming and warm place'. His mother had no doubt that 'that has contributed to Hamish's positive experiences with other children at school'.

Like Hamish, Ryan spent most of his break times playing sports with his friends. He named seven boys from his class with whom he regularly played sports, including two who were his 'best friends'. He also had friends outside school, extending from his family's friendships with other families. Ryan's mother described him as having:

> ...one quite close friend who has been his friend since he started at school, and three or four other good friends as well in his class. He has a couple of other friends in another class where he goes for extension work, and another friend, Max, who sticks up for him in the playground, he's got a real ally in him.

Ryan's mother did worry at times that his friends might get sick of his 'intense' behaviour when he was upset, 'because Ryan does have more things to be upset about than others'. But this had not been an issue:

> His reactions are very intense at times, but they seem to cope. He's learned to just go off when he's like that and come back to his friends when it's over. They kind of accept that too.

Although Ryan keenly participated in sport, his strengths lie in more academic areas. His mother was 'thrilled' that other children acknowledged these strengths, 'that these [academic] things are good and it's OK if you're a boy, you can be good at that, isn't that cool. I'm thrilled to see that.' In particular, one boy who had 'hassled' Ryan in the past had become one of his friends, and had written 'a really neat profile of a friend, and it was Ryan'.

Mike had two close friends in his class at secondary school. He also talked to a lot of the other students and participated in all the usual good-natured 'ribbing and hassling' of each other. He spent much of his out-of-school leisure time with his friends at each other's homes, playing on the Playstation. Mike's mother saw her role as supporting their visits to her home. She did not feel that the teachers had any role in Mike's developing or maintaining friendships and relationships with others at school. While this was not currently a problem, she did acknowledge that isolation had been a concern for Mike as a younger child. She suggested that the teachers at school would have known, but did not take any action to support Mike in this area.

Discussion

Friendship and relationship experiences at school varied considerably for the students with disabilities in our study. Ryan and Hamish at primary school and Mike at secondary school had close friends of similar age with whom they played both at school and at home, whereas Scott, Leah, Tom and Ben were socially isolated and had no close friends at all. They felt isolated, particularly at break times, and desperately wanted friends, but seemed unsure of how to go about getting them.

AJ and Andrew were well liked by others in the school because of their personalities and sense of humour, but they had not yet experienced the close supportive relationship of 'a best friend'. Leah (at intermediate school) and Aidan (in a Special Unit at secondary school) had friends who also had a disability. For Leah, this had raised some concerns about safety. The typical picture, then, is one of a lack of supportive peer relationships and friendships, a finding that is consistent with Traustadottir's (1993) point that children and adults with disabilities continue to be isolated and lonely and to have few friends.

While the nature of the children's friendships and relationships at school reflected their individual complexity and uniqueness, there were other factors that impacted on their relationships with other children. The school, as a social institution, has an overwhelmingly significant influence on the quality of social experiences. Its physical environment, children, teachers, other professionals, policy and ethos all contribute to that influence (Baker and Donelly, 2001). Like the parents in Baker and Donelly's study, most of the parents in our study tried to engineer and support friendships at home, but seemed unsure of what could and should be done in the school setting.

Placing a priority on friendships

Many parents in the study were aware that their children did not have 'real' friends, but this was rarely raised as a matter of concern with their children's teachers. Ben's mother seemed unsure about her son's friendships at school, and acknowledged that she didn't want to look when she walked past the school playground. She wondered about the social impact of removing Ben from the classroom. Some parents felt that it was not necessarily the task of the school to focus on friendships, while others seemed unsure of what could be expected for their children. Leah's mother, on the other hand, had raised the issue of friendships during her IEP, describing this as the only 'niggle' she had with the teacher. She was pleased that the teacher had since tried to encourage friendships by setting up a buddy system in Leah's class.

This general lack of attention to friendships at school might suggest that social goals are valued less than other learning goals for children with disabilities. Baker and Donelly (2001) found, for example, that academic and behavioural goals were valued more than social goals at school, and that social needs were considered 'something that can take care of itself' (p.80). Yet for most of the students we talked to, social experiences did not take care of themselves. They were affected by a whole range of environmental factors, and the school environment was highly influential in this process.

Placing priority on friendships and supportive relationships is critical for all children at school. This involves an appreciation of the developmental and learning impact of having no friends (George and Browne, 2000). Inclusive schools that teach diverse student groups create opportunities for children to learn important social norms, receive emotional support and security, and acquire the interpersonal foundations for later relationships (Salisbury and Palombaro, 1998). Friendships are critical to the development of all children (Smith, 1998a), and there is some evidence that social relationships at school can have a significant and broad impact on learning. While friendships and supportive relationships promote children's development, relationships that are not going well prevent students from focusing on their academic learning (George and Browne, 2000; Alton-Lee and Nuthall, 1992).

The social relationships of children with disabilities should receive attention at school and should be a focus of the IEP process. Discussions about friendships are most appropriately based on what is already known about friendship development for all children. In this context, teachers might critically examine the values and practices in their own schools that contribute to exclusion and loneliness (MacArthur and Morton, 1999). It is important, then, for teachers and other professionals to differentiate between fostering friendships (where the responsibility is on the school to develop pro-social environments) and 'social skills training' (where responsibility is placed on children with disabilities to change by teaching them skills that will enable them to interact with other children).

School ethos

Baker and Donelly (2001, p.81) refer to the school ethos as 'the distinctive climate, spirit and feeling of a place' which affects all children, but can compound problems for children with disabilities. In their ethnographic study they identified two types of school ethos: one of 'clemency' (conducive to social experiences) and one of 'tyranny' (deleterious to social experiences). In an ethos of clemency, teacher-student relationships were characterised by empathic emotional regard, propensity to care, mutual respect, discipline considerate of social consequences, and infrequent misbehaviour by children. In an ethos of tyranny, such relationships were characterised by apathetic emotional regard, lack of concern and respect, displays of hostility, discipline inconsiderate of social consequences, and periodic misbehaviour by children. The school ethos sets the scene for everything else that happens.

Some parents described school environments that were socially unsafe for their children. A school whose ethos does not foster positive relationships is less likely to worry about the isolation of children within the classroom, as Hamish and AJ experienced as five-year-olds in their first school. When teachers decided to 'protect' Tom from bullying by removing him from the playground (and thus from his peers), the relationship problem was interpreted as being his, and not belonging to the wider social environment of the school. Since proximity to peers is a fundamental requirement for children to develop friendships (Smith, 1998a), these examples suggest that some teachers see children with disabilities as 'deviant' and different from their peers. In supporting children's relationships, teachers need to reflect on where the responsibility for change should lie. If teachers are motivated by a *deficit model of disability*, the child with the disability will be seen as the problem. They may be blamed and excluded, like Tom, AJ and Hamish, or they may become the focus for change.

In contrast, a *social model of disability* argues that children's social contexts shape their social experiences (Oliver, 1996). This approach focuses on the relationship as involving two or more people, each with responsibilities and each participating within the broader social context of the school. Some parents in our study identified schools that had a supportive, warm and welcoming atmosphere. Hamish's second school, a small rural school, was one of these. AJ was 'just one of the kids' in his second school, and Leah had been involved in all activities at her small rural primary school. Parents identified the principal as a crucial person in establishing and maintaining this supportive environment, a point reiterated by Baker and Donelly (2001):

> The role of the principal in shaping the school milieu and the quality of social experiences is widely established... Parents believed that principals have significant power to remove some of the barriers to positive social experiences for children with disability. (p.76)

Teachers may not know what to do

Leah's mother recognised the challenges faced by parents and teachers when she described the issue of isolation and what to do about it as 'the hardest thing'. After she raised her concerns about friendship at Leah's IEP meeting, the teacher set up a buddy system and a roster for the other children to meet Leah at the school gate each morning. While these initiatives increased Leah's social contact with her peers, after six months no 'real friendships' had emerged. Leah's mother recognised that friendships could not be forced, but continued to look at other pro-social strategies with the teacher. Buddy systems are not uncommon in schools. However, they are inappropriate as a strategy for promoting friendships, as they usually involve formal relationships that lack spontaneity (Baker and Donelly, 2001). Meyer et al. (1998) remind us that friendships should not be confused with unequal relationships based on 'helping'. In contrast, peer tutoring systems that give students some opportunity to be spontaneous and enjoy each other's company may provide greater potential for friendships to develop (Baker and Donelly, 2001).

While Leah's teacher did actively intervene, Tom's school did not respond to his lack of friends. Scott's teacher aide tried some strategies to ensure that he would be present in the classroom when others were around, but the complexities of his disability meant that he spent break times alone. Scott did not have a teacher aide present to facilitate social interactions with other students over these long, unstructured periods, although his mother had advocated for this support to be made available. She acknowledged that he 'really hates break times'.

Meyer (2001) suggests that adults can and do play an important role in 'mediating' relationships, and that this role can result in facilitated, blocked or missed opportunities for social interactions. Teacher aides played an important role as mediators for some of the students in our study. Those who were well liked by other students (as in the case of Scott and Andrew) used their lively personalities and love of sports to engage other students in activities. Richard's teacher aide, on the other hand, was described by his brother as 'walking around with Richard' at break times. Meyer warns that a teacher aide who is 'velcroed at the hip' can block or prevent peer interactions and thus opportunities to develop friendships. In a New Zealand classroom, Philips (1997) found that students actively sought out moments when they could count on the teacher aide being absent so they could interact with their classmate with a disability and figure out ways for that student to participate.

Adults who facilitated peer interactions, on the other hand, were adept at recognising and responding to the teaching moment. Hamish's teachers in his small rural school recognised that he sometimes needed support to maintain positive relationships with his peers. They helped by becoming involved in games in the playground and smoothing the way with his peers where necessary. They also responded with empathy and respect to Hamish's own calls for assistance, and did not, as his mother had feared, see him as a 'tell-tale'. Similarly, Scott's teacher aide was skilful at identifying classroom situations where Scott would 'exclude himself', and worked with Scott to ensure that he was in the classroom at times when social engagement with his peers was most likely to happen.

'Real' friendships?

As well as considering the various contributions made to friendships by factors such as proximity and shared activities (Smith, 1998a), it is useful to consider how these factors might combine to create different levels of friendship. Meyer (2001) describes various 'frames' or understandings of friendship, where students with disabilities are considered by other students to be anywhere on a continuum from 'best friends' (a highly desirable frame) through to 'ghost/guests' (an undesirable frame) in the social environment of the classroom.

Our understanding of what is possible, rather than desired, in the relationships of children with disabilities is complicated by our understanding of how friendships develop for children without disabilities. Some parents acknowledged that their children did not have 'best' or 'close' friends, but stressed that they did not feel isolated because there was always someone to play with (a sibling's friend, a younger child, a 'part-time' friend). The prospect of having 'best friends' seemed an uncertain one.

Yet fifteen-year-old Scott demonstrated that it was possible to change one's own perspective on friendships when he indicated that he was now 'ready to have friends'. Similarly Mike, who had few friends at primary school, had several close friends at secondary school; and Hamish, who had no friends in his first school, had lots of friends at his new rural school. These experiences suggest that teachers and other adults need to remain open to the potential for students with disabilities to have close relationships with others, and to ensure that the social environment is able to support the development of those relationships.

If ten-year-old Richard's preference is for parallel play alongside younger children with a similar interest in toy cars, then teachers might support his development by building up his repertoire of interests and social skills. Alongside this process there are opportunities for Richard's peers to develop their own understandings and expectations of him. Meyer (2001) describes the four variables in this scenario (the repertoire of the child with a disability, the repertoire of their peers, the adult mediation, and the social ecology of the environment in which it occurs) as being associated with the building of social relationships. Friendship development can be maximised when all of these variables make complementary contributions.

'I don't know their names' – the impact of the student's disability

Some students in the study indicated that although they wanted to have friends, they had trouble working out just how to find them. While we would emphasise above all the role of the school environment in determining the social experiences of students with disabilities, the *nature* of each student's disability also placed constraints on their capacity to be socially engaged with their peers. Tom longed for the support and protection of friends, but his physical disability meant that he could not always keep up with his peers, and access at other people's homes was often a problem.

Leah too wanted friends and had tried to find friends from another class; but as she pointed out, she did not know their names. Her vision impairment made it virtually impossible for her to participate in the reciprocal non-verbal signs that go along with friendship development; it was also difficult to get to know other children in the school when she could not see them. Scott's autism spectrum disability made it hard for him to be part of a social group, and to respond in the usual way to other students' social initiatives. AJ was happiest when he was playing alongside other children, and he found it difficult to be too close to others.

While adults need to remain open to the possibility of close relationships for students with disabilities, they may also need to remain alert and sensitive to those aspects of a student's disability that make the development of such relationships difficult. This means listening with care and respect to the previously 'unfamiliar voices' of students with disabilities and their parents as they share their perspectives and experiences; it also means giving those voices a primary place when decisions are made about curriculum and teaching (Corbett, 1999). In relation to interactions with students, Corbett stresses that this involves a 'reciprocal process of mutual learning...it is about teachers *listening* rather than teachers *talking*' (p.56). In relation to interactions with parents, Ryan's mother expressed the following view near the end of her interview:

> I would hope that when I talk to teachers about specific issues in relation to his disability that they would show some understanding of the impact of his disability in general... of how how he feels about himself, how he sees himself. I would like teachers to have an awareness of how the disability actually affects that person's perception of themselves and how it affects them when they interact with other people.

Thinking broadly about what constitutes a positive social relationship for students might help teachers to define friendship in ways that are personal to the student and take into account the nature of their disability. Scott and AJ need to feel comfortable in their relationships with others, and should not be forced into relationships that are determined by others who do not understand their disability.

The emphasis in this book has been on supporting relationships with peers. It is important to recognise that the 'peer group' can be diverse in some schools, and may include other students with disabilities. Friendships are most likely to develop where students share interests and experiences. Some students may develop and enjoy relationships with others who have the same view of the world (as in autism spectrum disability), mode of communication, or method of mobility.

This point should not be misconstrued as support for segregated education. Such an interpretation would go against the overwhelming research and other support for inclusive education. It does suggest, however, that adults who support students with disabilities should be sensitive to the students' own preferences when considering opportunities for friendship development. For some students, particularly adolescents, this might mean exploring further opportunities for friendships beyond the school.

Teachers need to get to know each student and their family well, and be prepared to think about the potential impact of the child's disability on friendship development. This could mean considering ways to compensate for the disability, or adapting the school environment (both physical and social) to minimise its impact. Ryan's mother described the way his friends had learned how to respond to Ryan when he became 'intense', and Ryan had talked to his class about the impact his disability had on him. Scott's teachers might benefit from learning about the way students with autism spectrum disabilities understand their social world, and use that knowledge to inform their teaching. Leah's teachers may need to consider subtle and natural ways for her to meet other children in the school. In Tom's case, his teachers may need to help him experience proximity with his peers, shared interests, and supportive interactions that do not rely on being able to move fast around the playground. Attwood (2000) illustrates this process for students with Asperger Syndrome (part of the spectrum of autism disabilities). Students with this syndrome can actively look for friendship, but in a clumsy and not very successful way. They may have considerable difficulties in conceptualising and appreciating the thoughts of others, and find it hard to pick up on the relevant cues involved in social interchanges. Attwood suggests some strategies for encouraging social relationships, based on this understanding of the student's disability.

Families promoting friendships

Most of the parents in our study tried to engineer and support friendships between school and home by having other children home to play, maintaining close friendships and links with other families, or encouraging their children to participate in extracurricular activities, particularly sports. For Ryan, Hamish and Mike this was easy, because they had developed close friendships at school. Other families did not share this experience. AJ and Andrew played mostly with their siblings' friends, and rarely if ever had their own friends home to play. Others like Scott, Leah and Tom remained isolated both at school and at home.

Some of the parents in our study were not always able to support after-school friendships. In the case of Richard and Andrew, both parents worked during after-school hours. Other children had after-school activities, which in Tom's case made it difficult for him to establish relationships after school. It was not common for the children in this study to be involved in after-school activities, which can be an important environment for developing and cementing school friendships. It can be difficult for some parents to pursue after-school activities if their social supports are limited. As one parent said, 'life is just too busy'.

Transport and geography were problems for students like Leah and Tom who lived outside their school districts. It meant that home visits with children who lived in the local school community became even more difficult to arrange. While these are all factors that can affect children without disabilities, the presence of a disability may mean that a friend's parent is less likely to offer a lift home from school or to an after-school activity. Families who have a child with a disability usually encounter a range of additional stressors in their busy lives. While families are often resilient and positive, tiredness, stress and burnout can be a reality for many, and schools need to take this into account in their attempts to support friendships.

The relationship between friendships and bullying

Having friends does not necessarily prevent students with disabilities from being bullied, but friends may provide effective support and coping strategies for the student who is bullied. Ryan and his friends had devised a complex co-operative strategy to ensure that teachers were accurately informed about what had happened. Tom specifically recognised that friends could help him to deal with bullying. Rather than walking around the school on his own, he would 'like to play with my friends'. He suggested that some kids could stop the bullying by saying, 'Stop, that's my friend!'

Children with disabilities are likely to be victims of bullying on two counts. Isolated children are more likely to be bullied, because their isolation as well as their disability marks them as 'different'. They are also likely to lack the peer support that some children need to deal effectively with bullying. In this regard, they are doubly at risk of being victims. Friendships and supportive social relationships are not only critical to the healthy development of every child; they also provide schools with an important mechanism to foster a school-wide community in which bullying may cease to exist (Sullivan, 2000). This is a positive outcome for the whole school, not just for children with disabilities.

CHAPTER 4
Siblings, Bullying and Friendships

'Mitchell usually sticks up for Ryan...If anyone gets physical with Ryan, Mitchell will be there, pulling them off.'
(Mother of Ryan, aged eight, and Mitchell, aged five)

The relationship between siblings is special; not only is it usually the longest attachment most people have (Frank, 1996), but siblings also share important experiences. Most children with disabilities – Atkinson and Crawforth (1995) estimate about 80% – have non-disabled siblings. So it is important to recognise that a child's disability affects not only parents and caregivers but also brothers and sisters. Services and settings (including schools) that support children with disabilities and their families should therefore be sensitive to the needs of siblings as well.

Siblings of children with disabilities have some experiences that are unique to their position. For example, the literature repeatedly makes the point that brothers and sisters receive less attention from parents because of the additional caregiving needs of the child with a disability. Siblings, particularly sisters, also share the caregiving responsibilities undertaken by their parents (Burke and Montgomery, 2000). Siblings are generally aware that their situation is different from that of other children. They see both advantages and disadvantages in having a sibling with a disability: on the one hand, it can mean disruptions to their own social lives and opportunities; on the other, they may have more insights into the needs of others. Parents in Burke and Montgomery's study, for example, indicated that their non-disabled children were either more caring or more tolerant than other children.

While most children are resilient to the impact of their sibling's special needs, there are challenges associated with growing up in a family where a child has a disability. If the child has an autism spectrum disability, for example, siblings may need support to understand the nature of the disability, and to fit in with the balancing act that is family life (Harris, 1994). Siblings may also have to deal with other people's negative responses to their brother or sister, including teasing and bullying (Ellifrit, 1993; Harris, 1994; Klein and Schleiffer, 1993).

The siblings in our study who attended the same school as their disabled brother or sister were often very aware of their social experiences, and helped us to understand what these were. They usually knew that their brother or sister lacked friends, and knew if they were being bullied at school. Some described how they personally intervened to support their brother or sister when they were bullied, or when they were isolated and lonely. Others had a sense that things were not always going well for their brother or sister, but the geography of the school made it difficult to check this out. In contrast, some siblings seemed embarrassed by their brother or sister's behaviour, and not all felt able to offer support.

Siblings confronting bullying

Most siblings were aware that their brother or sister was a victim of bullying and actively intervened to prevent or stop bullying. In some situations, quite young siblings took on huge responsibilities by supporting their older brother or sister to confront bullying in the school playground.

Fifteen-year-old Aidan attended a Special Unit at secondary school. While bullying was not considered a problem in the wider school environment, Aidan had been bullied by other students in the unit. His older sister Kristin knew that Aidan and some of his peers were victims of bullying and were unable to protect themselves. Whenever possible she took on a protective role for her brother and others. She suggested that if physical bullying occurred at this school it was likely to involve students from the Special Unit, and that teachers were not often around when these things happened. She described breaking up a fight between three boys from the unit:

> I broke up a fight between them and this other poor boy. They were just picking on him, name-calling, starting to get physical, and I stepped in and stopped it…There were two [boys] and a lot bigger than this other kid and I thought, it's not right. I had to intervene there.

Two perpetrators were eventually excluded from the school, and Kristin felt that things had improved. Yet she worried that bullying remained an ongoing issue at school because 'they've just got more coming in [to the unit], starting it over again'. While she had not witnessed any physical bullying against Aidan, she had diffused some potentially difficult situations:

> I've just walked up to Aidan and said, 'What's going on?', and then [the bullies] sort of back-pedal and take off, [and I've] sent Aidan on his way with a friend.

Ryan's younger brother Mitchell, aged five, was in his first year at primary school. He described seeing Ryan being bullied by girls 'lots of times'. The interviewer asked him whether Ryan liked school:

Mitchell: Well, there is some really annoying girls come and tease him and I got some really annoying girls too.

Interviewer: What do the annoying girls do?
Mitchell: They tease us, really nasty stuff, 'buzz off' like, they say swear words.
Interviewer: Are these big girls or little girls.
Mitchell: Big girls...they swear at Ryan, they swear sometimes, they swear always...they kick him.

Mitchell said that the teachers at the school did talk about bullying:

Mitchell: They say [the bullies] have to stop it or they will have to go to another school, to a really really bullying school...Other kids think [bullying] is the right thing to do, but it's the wrong thing to do.
Interviewer: When you see kids bullying other children do you ever try to stop it yourself?
Mitchell: Yeah.
Interviewer: How do you feel when you see kids bullying other kids?
Mitchell: Sad.

Mitchell and Ryan's mother often stayed in the playground after school to support Ryan and to ensure that the other children let him join in their games. She frequently witnessed attempts to exclude him, and had heard some children refer to him as 'brainless'. She had also seen Mitchell supporting his older brother in this context:

> Mitchell usually sticks up for Ryan and if someone was verbally excluding Ryan [from a game] Mitchell would say very assertively, 'Yes, he can play, he can. Yes he can, so-and-so, he can come and play', or something like that. He can be very verbal and quite assertive...One time Ryan was just joining in and a younger boy came and got on top of him. It sort of looked like it was one of those rough-and-tumbles when it ended up getting quite rough and I was

just approaching to intervene and then Mitchell sort of picked up this boy and said, 'Hey, leave my brother. You do it to me but not my brother.' That was interesting...If anyone gets physical with Ryan, Mitchell will be there, pulling them off.

Twelve-year-old Peter was aware that some children did tease his younger brother Richard, who has Down Syndrome. He described an incident from 'about a year ago':

Peter: There's a couple of kids that just like to get into his personal space. And when he tells them to go away they won't – they'll just stay there.
Interviewer: So they're the same kids that we're talking about that do it again and again?
Peter: Sometimes, yes...
Interviewer: You haven't seen it happening this year, not that often?
Peter: Not any more.
Interviewer: Did something happen?
Peter: Oh, yes. Yes, I stopped it...It was Alistair's younger brother that was teasing him, and I just told him to go away.
Interviewer: And he hasn't done anything since?
Peter: No, not really, I haven't seen him. They're in different classes now, anyway.
Interviewer: So where does he like to play?
Peter: [In the playground] he has a teacher's aide that stays with him a lot. He just goes for walks...

Siblings helping with friendships and isolation

A number of siblings in the study showed they were aware of their brother or sister's relationships with others. Leah's younger sister Anna (aged eight) knew that Leah had few friends when they attended primary school together, saying that she 'used to play with the new entrants and that'. Anna did not know who could be described as Leah's 'best friends' because she 'mostly played with the little kids'. From the ages of five to seven, Anna had adopted a supportive role towards Leah. While she had never seen Leah being bullied at primary school, she added:

Anna: If she was, I'd just go, 'Well, sticks and stones may break her bones but names will never hurt her'.
Interviewer: You'd stick up for her.
Anna: Well, if it did happen, that is.

Anna would often seek Leah out at lunchtime and eat lunch with her, ensuring that she was not alone. She 'sometimes' played with Leah at playtime and lunchtime, recognising those moments when Leah seemed most in need of support:

Anna: Usually she would be playing with someone else. I'd only go up to her if she was on the computer and she was getting bored with the computer I'd go up and ask her to play.
Interviewer: I see. You would help her to come off the computer and go and do something else.
Anna: Yeah.
Interviewer: So that way she would have more fun and do different things, is that right?
Anna: Yep.

Hayley (aged eight) also described her brother Ben (aged six) as playing mostly with the little children (new entrants). She acknowledged that he could be lonely at school, because he sometimes looked serious when he came home.

While Kristin would actively intervene to protect her younger brother Aidan from bullying at high school, she did not become involved in his friendships with others. Yet she was very aware of the relationships Aidan had established at school, commenting that she would often see him pushing wheelchairs for other students in the Special Unit. She noted that while most of his time was spent in a small group of students with disabilities, she had also seen him 'hanging out with sixth-formers that are like in the "cool" group. They've taken him under their wing. If anyone is hassling him [they'll protect him].'

James (aged eleven), whose brother Scott (aged fifteen) has an autism spectrum disability, raised some different issues. James found it difficult to deal with some aspects of his brother's disability, and his mother saw his embarrassment as a reflection of his age and personality:

> Scott will walk around talking to himself and I'm fine about that, that's not a problem, but…James is at an age where he is just so embarrassed about things. He's so conscious of things and of course when Scott gets dressed in the morning half the things are on back-to-front and he doesn't even care. There's no image thing with him, but James is just into it. He's image conscious, but you see, having a brother like Scott doesn't fit it, for a kid who is becoming a teenager and very into image and doing the right thing…James is very much a perfectionist…he just wants to make the right impression, but his brother just can't do it…having a brother who stands out…he finds it really hard.

James worried about Scott being seen to be different in front of his own peers. His mother wondered if this had prevented James from bringing his own friends home:

> I've often wondered if that's why James won't invite friends to our place, especially new children who don't know Scott. I've said, 'Share phone numbers, bring them home, I'm quite happy for them to come home'. But he always finds an excuse not to. I just wonder whether it's because Scott is there or

what, because Scott is usually at home too. You know what I mean, and yet I think, 'bugger, it shouldn't matter'…but he is always worried about the worst. He wants to blend in and not be noticed and his brother doesn't blend in.

Siblings have needs too

The experiences and perspectives of the siblings in our study suggest that siblings have their own needs in the school context. Some siblings were concerned about their brother or sister being isolated or bullied. However, the siblings knew about their school's anti-bullying procedures and used them. They seemed unconcerned about discussing these matters with us, and dealt matter-of-factly with the issue of bullying. Mitchell's mother was pleased that although he was only five, he felt able to intervene and support his brother when he was teased or excluded, noting that he could be 'very verbal and quite assertive'.

It would be wrong, however, to conclude that siblings are not affected in some way by these experiences. The literature identifies the witnessing of teasing as a reality for many siblings. It suggests that being involved in such events can be traumatic, arousing a range of feelings from wanting to defend their sibling through to embarrassment at being associated with someone who is so different in the eyes of others (Harris, 1994; Klein and Schleiffer, 1993). Klein and Schleiffer suggest that there is an emotional cost. One of the siblings in their study, Tracy (aged thirteen), commented:

> I heard some guy down the back of the bus talking about Mark and how stupid he was, and you could make him do anything and he is so gullible, and all that kind of stuff. I walked back to the kid and slugged him in the face. I was getting really annoyed and he could not understand what

was happening. I always felt that I had to protect [Mark] from someone, from teasing, from fights, and any other kids trying to put one over on kids who are at a disadvantage to them. If you love somebody you cannot help but get emotionally involved in that. (p.8)

Similarly, Harris (1994) describes eight-year-old Dick Jansen's emotional response to some older boys who teased him about his 'dumb old [autistic] brother [who] acts so weird', then pushed him over:

> Dick began to choke with tears as the words flooded out to his father, 'What's wrong with Mal? Why won't he talk? Maybe he just doesn't want to. The guys are right, Daddy. He acts so weird sometimes. I just want him to be a regular brother. I know Mal has autism, but why does he have to be so weird? I stood up for him, but I don't understand why he is that way.' The words tumbled out until, out of breath and angry-sad, Dick finally stopped. (p.28)

Other siblings have described their embarrassment about their brother or sister with a disability, in much the same way that James expressed mixed feelings in our study (Klein and Schleiffer, 1993). Ellifrit (1993) graphically describes her childhood need to have her own identity, apart from her sister Bonnie, who was two years older and had Down Syndrome:

> During my grade school years I thought of Bonnie as a witch. She had long stringy hair and she was skinny. She drooled and twisted her fingers and had other unpleasant habits. My friends would come over to play, take one look at her, and some would actually turn around and leave...[As an adolescent] I wanted so much to be accepted by my peers, and yet no one would play with me because of my shadow – my 'social disease' that would not go away. The kids at school would tease, take advantage, and play tricks on her and the other 'special kids' in the lunchroom. (p.99)

Twenty-two years later she still 'lived with the guilt, but also with a better understanding of her experience, which had made her a more tolerant, understanding person'. In her family, Bonnie's disability was never discussed, and nor were her own feelings towards Bonnie:

> We were not allowed to discuss our feelings about Bonnie. After all, she was retarded and if we said anything negative, we might hurt her feelings. Well what about my feelings?... My parents never sat me down and said, 'There is this problem. This is what's wrong with her. Do you understand? Do you have any questions? (pp.98-9)

Dick Jansen also revealed that he understood very little about his brother's disability. But in contrast to Ellifrit's experience, his father realised that he should help Dick to understand what autism was, to feel confident in his factual information, and to handle the insults he might encounter on his brother's behalf.

Open discussion in the family about a child's disability may help siblings to deal with difficult playground situations. Teachers too may be able to support siblings by recognising that they have unique experiences and needs. But more importantly, if schools are to be supportive environments for all children, then principals, teachers and other staff need to take seriously the issues of isolation and bullying and their impact on children. Schools that are free from bullying (and some schools in our study were identified as such), and where children have friends, are safe places for children with disabilities *and* their siblings. While we might celebrate the fact that siblings can be so supportive, we should also ensure that schools are places where siblings are free to just be children, without carrying the responsibility for protecting their brothers and sisters with disabilities.

CHAPTER 5

Implications for Schools:

Creating Safe and Supportive School Environments for Students with Disabilities and their Siblings

We recently shared some of the findings from our study with the parents involved. In response to the question, 'What message would you want schools to take from this study', parents stressed that *it should not be their children who are always expected to change*. In their experience, bullying and friendship issues were interpreted as their child's problem. The onus was on the student with the disability to change to fit the school environment, rather than the reverse. This kind of thinking comes from a medical model in which disability is associated with deviance and difference (Oliver, 1992). Teachers who think about students with disabilities in this way will harbour values and engage in practices that exclude them.

Parents in the study felt strongly that other children in the school should also be expected to change to become more supportive of children with disabilities. Parents considered it vitally important that other children and teachers get to know their child in order to understand them and their experiences of isolation and bullying at school, so they can intervene in positive ways.

This is *not* an unreasonable expectation. The fostering of social relationships, by definition, involves more than one person, and other children can play a key role by learning about the child with the disability, understanding the impact of their disability, and playing a responsive, nurturing and supportive role, based on this understanding (Attwood, 2000; Meyer, 2001). Inclusion in education should encourage 'a gentler school climate in which children must and do learn to help and take care of one another both socially and academically' (L. M. Meyer, cited in Smith, 1998b).

Unlike the children with disabilities in some studies of social experiences, all but one student in our study had always been taught in the regular classroom. We can learn from the experiences of Mike, Ryan and Hamish, who all had friends. Nonetheless, we should emphasise that the majority of the students with disabilities had very unusual social experiences at school, characterised by bullying and loneliness. While proximity is fundamental to friendship development, the mainstream environment still has the capacity to exclude. Being *in* the mainstream, then, needs to be differentiated from being an integral member *of* the mainstream. We should also reflect on the impact these unusual social experiences might have on children's overall development, including their mental health and their learning. Loneliness, for example, has been associated with the development of poor self-esteem, increased anxiety and depression (Pavri, 2001). While links are suggested between bullying and both mental and physical health problems (Wolke et al., 2001).

The students and parents in our study have alerted us to some of the ways in which schools can foster supportive relationships between students with disabilities and their non-disabled peers. They have also identified barriers to achieving supportive social environments. This chapter considers some of the implications of the study for teachers and schools: *what* makes school environments pro-social for children with disabilities? Our discussion focuses on the role played by various people within the school environment.

School leadership, policy and curriculum

Leadership is important

The school principal has been identified both in the wider literature and by parents in our study as playing a key role in establishing, shaping and maintaining a supportive social environment in the school. As leaders, principals can set the scene for supportive relationships by promoting inclusive values and practices at all levels of the school. Principals also have the power to remove some of the barriers to positive social experiences for children with disabilities (Baker and Donelly, 2001). Parents in the study identified pro-social school environments as a direct extension of the principal's commitment to including children with disabilities alongside their non-disabled peers. Such schools were described as welcoming places with an inclusive ethos and strong community focus.

Conversely, some parents described difficulties in having their concerns about their child's social experiences heard at school. Parents need to feel free to approach their school principal if they have concerns, and should have some faith that those concerns will be addressed. Schools that value and support diversity in their students will also value the different perspectives and experiences of students and their parents. Change may be difficult to effect in schools where the principal is not committed to this fundamental principle of inclusion.

Support for relationships in national policy and the curriculum

At the level of national policy and curriculum, there is an emphasis on schools as safe and supportive environments for all children. In the National Administration Guidelines for New Zealand schools, NAG 5 states that each Board of Trustees is required to 'provide a safe physical and emotional environment for students'. While school policies may reflect the intention to meet this requirement, our study suggests that the implementation of policies, including those dealing with bullying, is dependent on a number of factors, including the school's culture and ethos. While some schools responded immediately to reports of bullying, some had a culture of secrecy or denial, and others treated bullying as a personal problem for students with disabilities.

Likewise, schools are required by the Health and Physical Education curriculum (Ministry of Education, 1999) to teach students to 'develop sensitivity to, and respect for, other people' and to 'use interpersonal skills effectively to enhance relationships'. The curriculum document (based on the Curriculum Framework, in which the rhetoric is pro-inclusion) has a strong emphasis on social well-being and relationships with other people. How these principles are put into practice in relation to children's understanding of disability and difference, and to children's social development, will be determined, once again, by the wider school ethos.

One way of assessing a school's ethos is through the self-review process that all schools are now required to undertake. Within this process, parents might ask questions such as:

Does my child feel safe at school?

Are all children treated fairly?

Are interactions between teachers and students and teachers and parents respectful?

Will my experience as a parent be valued?

If I have a concern about the school, do I know that someone will listen and respond appropriately?

Teachers, teacher aides and other school staff
Friendships are important

Some parents in our study seemed unsure about the role that schools could or should play in the development of children's friendships. Only one parent, for example, reported discussing the issue as part of the IEP process, although some parents played an active role in ensuring that their child was socially secure at school. Parents were generally not aware that ideas about supportive relationships were enshrined in the National Curriculum. Their comments suggested that social relationships may receive less attention than other aspects of their child's learning and development. Friendships and supportive social relationships, then, may not be regarded at school as a priority for students who have disabilities.

One explanation is that some teachers may attribute isolation to the child's disability, and thus see friendships as unrealistic and unimportant. Yet this conclusion is inconsistent with the child development literature, which stresses the important link between friendships and overall development and learning (Alton-Lee and Nuthall, 1992; Salisbury and Palombaro, 1998; Smith, 1998a). Blaming the child in this way can prevent teachers from seeing the importance of friendships for *all* children, including those with a disability, and may distract them from seeking positive changes in the wider school environment. This is an attitude that is readily challenged by focusing on friendships and relationships in pre-service teacher education and professional development, and by listening to parents' aspirations and concerns for their children.

Teachers are mediators of relationships

Adults in school environments are important mediators of their students' social experiences, who can facilitate, block or miss opportunities for social interaction (Meyer, 2001). Teachers can facilitate relationships by looking critically at the place of the student in the classroom (both physically and socially), and at their own teaching strategies. This includes scrutinising group work, peer-tutoring, buddy systems and classroom management procedures, and ensuring that they include opportunities for natural, enjoyable and spontaneous peer interactions. Teachers are also responsible for establishing clear roles and responsibilities for teacher aids in their classrooms. So teachers need to reflect on the extent to which the role and behaviour of teacher aides includes or excludes children with disabilities.

Listen to students and parents

In relation to bullying, the children and parents in our study expressed a common view that their experiences were not always understood or attended to. Some schools were described by parents and students as safe places where bullying simply would not happen, suggesting an 'ethos of clemency' as described by Baker and Donelly (2001). In other schools, the response of teachers to bullying was inconsistent, and students readily identified those who would be supportive and those who would do nothing. It was not easy for parents to report incidents of bullying, particularly when their child's behaviour was misunderstood and they were perceived to be the perpetrator rather than the victim, or were seen as 'whingeing'.

These points serve to highlight the unique experiences of children with disabilities and the complexities of the playground setting. Bullying for some children was frequent, personal and hurtful, and focused on their disability. It was often hidden from teachers and was therefore poorly understood. It is vital that teachers listen carefully and respectfully to the experiences and perspectives of students with disabilities and their parents. Only then will they fully understand the context in which bullying occurs, the impact it has on the student, and the solutions that might be sought.

Implicit in all these points is the need for mutually respectful and supportive partnerships between parents and teachers, in which the parents' valuable store of information can be used in productive ways. Parents with sons and daughters in highly supportive schools were free to communicate with staff, usually informally, on a daily basis. Ryan's mother had established a good relationship with his teacher, with whom she was often able to talk briefly and informally. She found it difficult, however, to arrange formal and extended meetings where she and Ryan's father could talk to the teacher about Ryan's school experience. Scheduling meeting times is a challenge for most busy teachers and parents, but the parents in our study emphasised the importance of being able to share information, air concerns, tackle problems, and make plans for their child's education.

Children with disabilities

Balancing skills with environments

Children with disabilities can and should learn skills that help them to develop social competencies. However, an over-emphasis on this as an approach to developing friendships places the responsibility squarely on the shoulders of the student with a disability. Schools play a significant role in determining children's relationships as they grow and develop. Wider environmental factors, such as the geography of the school, the school ethos, the values and practices of the principal, teachers and other adults, and the understandings and behaviour of peers, should be the primary focus for change.

Within this responsive context, teachers need to listen respectfully to students with disabilities in order to understand their social experiences at school and the impact of their disability. This knowledge can then be used in planning and teaching. One positive outcome of working in this way is the building of resilience in children who may already be challenged by the personal and wider impact of their disability. Supportive schools can build self-esteem, promote a strong sense of identity, and build skills that will protect the children as they move into new social environments (Gilligan, 2001).

Children's rights

New Zealand schools are increasingly recognising the need to address the rights of children, as enshrined in The United Nations Convention on the Rights of the Child (UNCROC), to which New Zealand is a signatory. UNCROC provides another context in which to understand the school's role in supporting children with disabilities. While Article 23 refers specifically to children with disabilities, it is important to remember that the *whole* Convention applies to them, thus establishing their right to be viewed as a child first and foremost (Bray and Gates, 2000; Hammarberg, 1995).

Article 12 (1) establishes the right of every child to have their views respected, yet the children in our study had mixed experiences in this regard. Some had a voice in the school, just like any other child; but others, like Tom, felt powerless to do anything about bullying and isolation because teachers did not always respond to his reports and concerns. Article 6 (2) covers the right to physical, mental, emotional, cognitive, social and cultural development. Article 23 stresses that a disabled child shall enjoy 'a full and decent life in conditions which ensure dignity, promote self-reliance and facilitate the child's active participation in the community'. This article aims not only to give children with disabilities the same rights as other children, but also to ensure that they have real and concrete possibilities to exercise those rights (Hammarberg, 1995). Some children in our study did experience such conditions, but for others the right to dignity and active participation in their school community remained a dream.

As schools move towards a recognition of children's rights, it will be important for staff and Boards of Trustees to remember that the Convention is designed to protect *all* children. The articles may then serve as a reminder to schools that children with disabilities may be particularly vulnerable to having their rights ignored or abused.

Peers

'Just another kid'

Peers within the school form the other part of the relationship equation. Their own understandings about disability and the place of students with disabilities in the school community will contribute to the social experiences of those students. Some students in our study were valued by their peers as class members, as 'just another kid' in the school. Such relationships readily extended from the classroom into the playground and sometimes to home.

Giving peers the skills and opportunities to interact

Some teachers supported students with disabilities and their peers by participating in games, and intervening when necessary in challenging social situations. They used their knowledge of the child with a disability to educate their peers, and to give them skills for interacting with and supporting students with disabilities. These strategies were designed to support relationships and friendship development. Leah's teacher introduced a roster for meeting Leah at the school gate so that she too could enter school in the company of her peers, rather than alone. While this had not yet resulted in real friendships, it became an important starting point for Leah's classmates to get to know her. Ryan and his mother had also worked with the class teacher to ensure that peers knew about his disability and could understand the social and other challenges he occasionally faced. This knowledge was empowering for the peers who knew him well, because they knew how to respond supportively if Ryan became 'too intense' in his interactions with them.

Identifying barriers

Some teachers placed barriers in the way of friendships between students with disabilities and their peers. This suggests that they needed to reflect critically on the potential of their own values and actions to exclude some children. Games in which there are distinct 'winners' and 'losers' gave some peers the opportunity to pick on children with disabilities. Blaming the victims of bullying rather than the perpetrators, or ignoring bullying altogether, delivers a powerful message to peers that disability is associated with deviance and difference, rather than sameness and belonging. Buddy systems may be based on formal 'helping' relationships that lack spontaneity. Having a 'velcroed' teacher aide can reduce opportunities for students with disabilities to interact with their peers.

Families and siblings

Parents deserve a life

The importance of establishing and maintaining a respectful and reciprocal partnership between school and family has already been discussed. Within this context, however, parents need to know what their role is in relation to the school. Some parents in our study were expected to commit themselves to a part-time, unpaid job as support to the school. At his first school, AJ's mother was expected to take him home every lunchtime, pick him up every afternoon at 2 pm, and personally assist him at swimming while seven months pregnant.

No other parent has these responsibilities placed on them. Yet parents of children with disabilities may find it hard to say 'no' in case there is a backlash against their child. Schools should not place unrealistic expectations on these parents. Nor should they expect the parents to be grateful to the school for teaching their child. Parents and teachers need to work together to establish a level of parental involvement that is comfortable and appropriate to support the student's development and learning. At the same time, schools need to recognise that some parents may be exhausted by the day-to-day tasks and demands associated with caring for a child with a disability, particularly where there are few social supports available.

Parents also bring to any situation a healthy emotional involvement with their child. AJ's mother described this intensely personal experience:

> I don't think that schools realise what parents go through when your kiddy's [disabled]…you try to let go but you're

just so protective of them because you are so open to things going wrong for them. You really want to care for them, it's really hard to just not. It's not like your other children, you send them off to school and things will be right or if they're not you'll be told. I don't think people realise what parents go through when you're changing schools or moving on from one place to another.

Schools need to realise that the parents' involvement with their child's education may have been shaped by numerous experiences of exclusion. A challenge for teachers and principals is to consider ways in which their school might turn this experience around.

Looking after the brothers and sisters

Siblings may also have additional responsibilities in families where a child has a disability. Some siblings in our study took on responsibilities beyond their years to ensure that their brother or sister with a disability was physically safe and socially secure. While it is important for schools to bear in mind the unique needs of these children, schools that commit themselves to eliminating bullying, removing barriers to friendships, and working to make their wider school environment inclusive will be doing a favour not only to students with disabilities but also to their siblings.

Conclusion

Children with disabilities, their parents and siblings willingly shared with us their perspectives and experiences of social relationships at school. We must acknowledge that this process was sometimes difficult as parents and children relived challenging situations they felt powerless to change. But they also shared success stories. Some families experienced new hope as they watched their children develop friendships in welcoming and supportive schools that were characterised by a genuine commitment to inclusion.

The small group of children and parents in our study have made a huge contribution to our understanding of safe and unsafe, supportive and unsupportive school contexts in which children develop socially. We have written this book because their voices have the potential to make New Zealand schools into better, safer, more supportive places for students with disabilities.

References

Adair, V., Dixon, R., Moore, D. and Sutherland, R. (1998). *Ask your mother not to make yummy sandwiches: Bullying in New Zealand secondary schools.* Centre for Child and Family Policy, University of Auckland.

Adair, V. (1999). No bullies at this school: Creating safer schools. *Childrenz Issues, 3,* 32-37.

Alton-Lee, A. and Nuthall, G. (1992). Students learning in classrooms: Curricular, instructional and sociocultural processes influencing student interactions with curriculum content. Paper presented to AERA conference in San Francisco.

Amado, A. (1993). *Friendship and community connections between people with and without disabilities.* Baltimore: Paul Brookes Publishing Co.

Atkinson, N. and Crawforth, M. (1995). *All in the family: Siblings and disability.* London: NCH Action for Children.

Attwood, T. (2000). Strategies for improving the social integration of children with Asperger syndrome. *Autism, 4,* (1), 85-100.

Baker, K. and Donelly, M. (2001). The social experiences of children with disability and the influence of environment: A framework for intervention. *Disability and Society, 16,* (1), 71-85.

Ballard, K. (1998). Disability and discrimination: Laws, ethics and practices. *Childrenz Issues, 2,* (2), 27-30.

Bogdan, R. and Taylor, S. (1992). The social construction of humanness: Relationships with severely disabled people. In P. M. Ferguson and S. J. Taylor (Eds.), *Interpreting Disability.* New York: Teachers College Press.

Brantlinger, E. (1997). Using ideology: Cases of nonrecognition of the politics of research and practice in special education. *Review of Educational Research, 67,* (4), 425-429.

Bray, A. and Gates, S. (2000). Children with disabilities: Equal rights or different rights? In A. Smith, M. Gollop, K. Marshall and K. Nairn (Eds.), *Advocating for children: International perspectives on children's rights.* Dunedin: University of Otago Press.

Burke, P. and Montgomery, S. (2000). Siblings of children with disabilities: A pilot study. *Journal of Learning Disabilities, 4,* (3), 227-236.

Corbett, J. (1999). Inclusive education and school culture. *International Journal of Inclusive Education, 3,* (1), 53-61.

Cresswell, J. W. (1994). *Research design: Qualitative and quantitative approaches.* London: Sage Publications.

Ellifrit, J. (1993). Life with my sister: Guilty no more. In S. Klein and M. Schleiffer (Eds.), *It isn't fair! Siblings of children with disabilities.* Westport, Connecticut: Bergin & Garvey.

Evans, I., Salisbury, C., Palombaro, M., Berryman, J. and Hollowood, T. (1992). Peer interactions and social acceptance of elementary-age children with severe disabilities in an inclusive school. *Journal of the Association for Persons with Severe Handicaps, 17,* (4), 205-212.

Frank, N. (1996). Helping families support siblings. In P. J. Beckman (Ed.), *Strategies for working with families of children with disabilities.* Baltimore, MD: Brookes.

George, R. and Browne, N. (2000). 'Are you in or are you out?' An exploration of girl friendship groups in the primary phase of schooling. *International Journal of Inclusive Education, 4,* (4), 289-300.

Gilligan, R. (2001). *Promoting resilience: A resource guide on working with children in the care system.* London: British Agency for Adoption and Fostering.

Hall, L. (1994). A descriptive assessment of social relationships in integrated classrooms. *Journal of the Association for Persons with Severe Handicaps, 19,* (4), 302-313.

Hammarberg, T. (1995). The rights of disabled children: The UN Convention on the Rights of the Child. In T. Degener and Y. Koster-Dreese (Eds.), *Human rights and disabled persons: Essays and relevant human rights instruments.* Dordrecht, The Netherlands: Martinus Kijhoff Publishers.

Harris, S. (1994). *Siblings of children with autism: A guide for families.* Bethesda, MD: Woodbine House.

Klein, S. and Schleiffer, M. (1993). *It isn't fair! Siblings of children with disabilities.* Westport, Connecticut: Bergin & Garvey.

Lutfiyya, Z. (1990). *Affectionate bonds: What we can learn by listening to friends.* Syracuse, NY: Center on Human Policy, Syracuse University.

MacArthur, J. and Morton, M. (1999). 'I'm still trying to make friends...': Fostering and nurturing the development of friendships and supportive relationships in inclusive schools. *Childrenz Issues, 3,* (1), 38-42.

Maeroff, G. I. (1998). Altered destinies: Making life better for school children in need. *Phi Delta Kappan,* February, 425-432.

Maharaj, A. S., Tie, W. and Ryba, K. (2000). Deconstructing bullying in Aotearoa/New Zealand: Disclosing its liberal and colonial connections. *New Zealand Journal of Educational Studies, 35* (1), 9-23.

Maxwell, G. and Lind, J. (1996). *Children's experience of violence.* Wellington: Office of the Commissioner for Children.

Meyer, L., Minondo, S., Fisher, M., Larson, M., Dunmore, S., Black, J. and D'Aquanni, M. (1998). Frames of friendship: Social relationships among adults with diverse abilities. In L. Meyer, H. Park, M. Grenot-Sheyer, I. Schwartz and B. Harry (Eds.), *Making friends: The influence of culture and development.* Ohio: Paul H. Brookes Publishing Co.

Meyer, L. (2001). The impact of inclusion on children's lives: Multiple outcomes, and friendships in particular. *International Journal of Disability, Development and Education, 48,* (1), 9-31.

Ministry of Education (1999). *Health and physical education in the New Zealand Curriculum.* Wellington: Learning Media.

Mooney, S. and Smith, P. K. (1995). Bullying and the child who stammers. *British Journal of Special Education, 22,* (1), 24-27.

Murray-Seegert, C. (1989). *Nasty girls, thugs, and humans like us: Social relations between severely disabled and nondisabled students in high school.* New York: Paul H. Brooks Publishing Co.

Oliver, M. (1992). Intellectual masturbation: A rejoinder to Soder and Booth. *European Journal of Special Needs Education, 7,* (1), 20-28.

Oliver, M. (1996). *Understanding disability: From theory into practice.* Basingstoke: McMillan.

Pavri, S. (2001). Loneliness in children with disabilities: How teachers can help *Teaching Exceptional Children, 33,* (6) 52-58.

Philips, R. J. (1997). Social interactions and social relationships between children with and without disabilities: Shifting the focus. Unpublished MA thesis, University of Canterbury.

Pitman, A. and Maxwell, J. A. (1992). Qualitative approaches to evaluation. In M. D. LeCompte, W. L. Millroy and J. Preissle (Eds.), *The handbook of qualitative research in education.* London: Academic Press.

Purdue, K., Ballard, K. and MacArthur, J. (2001). Exclusion and inclusion in New Zealand early childhood education: Disability, discourses and contexts. *International Journal of Early Years Education, 9,* (1), 37-49.

Purdue, K., MacArthur, J. and Ballard, K. (1998). Inclusion in early childhood education as early intervention. *Proceedings of the Australian Early Intervention Third Biennial Conference, Sydney, 3-5 September 1998.*

Salisbury, C. L. and Palombaro, M. M. (1998). Friends and acquaintances: Evolving relationships in an inclusive elementary school. In L. Meyer, H. Park, M. Grenot-Sheyer, I. Schwartz and B. Harry (Eds.), *Making friends: The influence of culture and development.* Ohio: Paul H. Brookes Publishing Co.

Sapon-Shevin, M., Dobbelaere, A., Corrigon, C., Goodman, K. and Mastin, M. C. (1998). Promoting inclusive behaviour in inclusive classrooms: 'You can't say you can't play'. In L. Meyer, H. Park, M. Grenot-Sheyer, I. Schwartz and B. Harry (Eds.). *Making friends: The influence of culture and development.* Ohio: Paul H. Brookes Publishing Co.

Schnorr, R. (1990). 'Peter? He comes and goes...': First graders' perspectives on a part-time mainstream student. *Journal of the Association for Persons with Severe Handicaps, 15,* (4), 231-240.

Schwandt, T. (1994). Constructivist, interpretivist approaches to human inquiry. In N. Denzin and Y. Lincoln (Eds.), *Handbook of qualitative research.* Thousand Oaks, CA: Sage Publications.

Skrtic, T. M. (1986). The crisis in special education knowledge: A perspective on perspective. *Focus on Exceptional Children, 18,* (7), 1-16.

Skrtic, T. M. (1995). *Disability and democracy: Restructuring (special) education for postmodernity*. New York: Teachers College Press.

Smith, A. B. (1998a). *Understanding children's development: A New Zealand perspective*. Wellington: Bridget Williams Books.

Smith, A. (1998b). Introduction – Postmodern pedagogy: Toward a kinder, gentler nation? In L. Meyer, H. Park, M. Grenot-Sheyer, I. Schwartz and B. Harry (Eds.), *Making friends: The influence of culture and development*. Ohio: Paul H. Brookes Publishing Co.

Smith, P. K. and Sharp, S. (1994). *School bullying: Insights and perspectives*. London: Routledge.

Strully J. and Strully, C. (1992). The struggle towards inclusion and the fulfilment of friendship. In N. Nisbet (Ed.), *Natural supports in school, at work and in the community for people with severe disabilities*. Ohio: Paul H. Brookes Publishing Co.

Sullivan, K. (2000). *The anti-bullying handbook*. Auckland: Oxford University Press.

Taylor, S. and Bogdan, R. (1989). On accepting relationships between people with mental retardation and non-disabled people: Towards an understanding of acceptance. *Disability, Handicap and Society, 4*, (1), 21-36.

Torrance, D. A. (1997). 'Do you want to be in my gang?': A study of the existence and effects of bullying in a primary school class. *British Journal of Special Education, 24*, (4), 158-162.

Torrance, D. A. (2000). Qualitative studies into bullying within special schools. *British Journal of Special Education, 27*, (1), 16-21.

Traustadottir, R. (1993). The gendered context of friendships. In A. Amado (Ed.), *Friendship and community connections between people with and without disabilities*. Baltimore: Paul Brookes Publishing Co.

Watson, M., Holton, D. and Andrew, S. (1999). *Children with autism: Suggestions for teaching in the inclusive classroom*. Dunedin: Donald Beasley Institute Inc.

Whitney, I., Smith, P. K. and Thompson, D. (1994). Bullying and children with special educational needs. In P. K. Smith and S. Sharp, *School bullying: Insights and perspectives*. London: Routledge.

Wolke, D., Woods, S., Bloomfield, L., and Karstadt, L. (2001) Bullying involvement in primary school and common health problems. *Archives of Disease in Childhood, 85,* (3), 197-209.

Zetlin, A. and Murtaugh, M. (1988). Friendship patterns of mildly learning handicapped and non-handicapped high school students. *American Journal of Mental Retardation, 92,* 447-454.

Index

Adair, V., 7, 13
Alton-Lee, A., 72, 97
Amado, A., 10
Atkinson, N., 83
Attwood, T., 80, 94

Ballard, K., 10, 12
Baker, K., 71-73, 74, 95, 98
Brantlinger, 47
Bray, A., 8, 100
Browne, N., 72
Bogdan, R., 10, 47
bullying
  active, 13
  'blaming the victim' 32, 44, 48, 49, 73, 98, 102
  forms of, 14, 44
  friends involvement, 37, 38, 41, 45, 76
  hidden, 44
  long-term developmental impacts of, 7, 94
  non-physical /emotional, 14, 20, 44
  non-verbal, 14
  parents' strategies to deal with, 28, 29, 32, 58, 62, 92, 93, 99, 103, 104
  patterns, 43
  perpetrators of, 20-22, 25, 26, 43, 44, 102
  physical, 14, 20, 22, 26, 30, 33-34, 43, 44, 85
  schools' strategies to deal with, 13, 20, 25, 26, 28-42, 46-50, 65, 73, 90-96, 98, 99, 101
  students' strategies to deal with, 38-42, 49, 82
  talk, walk, squawk, 37, 42, 49
  verbal, 14, 23, 24-27, 30, 41, 44, 45, 85-87, 90
Burke, P., 83

Children's Issues Centre, 8, 17, 115
children's rights, 100, 101
Corbett, J., 47, 79
Crawforth, M., 83
Cresswell, J. W., 15

Donald Beasley Institute, 8, 17, 115
Donelly, M., 71-73, 74, 95, 98
disabilities
  Asperger Syndrome, 80
  associated with deviance, 47, 93, 102
  autism spectrum, 22, 35, 38, 52, 78-80, 84, 92
  co-ordination difficulties, 25
  deficit model of, 74
  Down Syndrome, 34, 64, 91
  intellectual, 22, 23, 45
  learning and behavioural, 61
  low vision, 26-27, 56
  mild or moderate, 12
  physical and learning, 26,
  severe, 12
  social model of, 74

Ellifrit, J., 84, 91, 92
environments (*see also* social relationships), 12, 92, 93, 94, 95, 97, 98, 100, 104
exclusion (*see* isolation)

Evans, I., 12, 43

friendships, 7, 8, 9, 51, 71, 72, 76, 77, 79, 82, 94, 97, 99, 102
  components of, 9
  facades of, 10
  families promoting, 81-82
  'real', 67-69, 70, 75, 76
  reciprocal, 10, 11
  unequal, 10

Gaffney, M., 8
Gates, S., 100
George, R., 71, 72
Gilligan, R., 100
Gollop, M, 8

Hall, L., 11
Hammarberg, T., 100, 101
Harris, S., 84, 90, 91
Health and Physical Education Curriculum, 9, 96

inclusion, 46, 47, 72, 104, 105
integration, 47
interpretivist approach, 15
intimidatory practices, 15
isolation, 7, 10, 13, 15, 28, 44-47, 51-57, 62-65, 70, 74, 82, 90, 92, 93, 97
  categories of, 51
  impacts of, 72, 79
  schools' strategies to deal with, 54-56, 58-59, 62, 64, 66, 71, 72, 80, 98, 102
  students' strategies to deal with, 60-61, 63-64, 66

Klein, S., 84, 90, 91

Lind, J., 13
Lutfiyya, Z., 10

MacArthur, J., 7, 8, 10
Maeroff, G. I., 46
Maharaj, A. S., 15, 45
Maxwell, G., 13
Meyer, L., 10, 75-77, 94, 98
Montgomery, S., 83
Mooney, S., 12, 43
Morton, M., 7
Murtaugh, M., 11
Murray-Seegert, C., 10

name-calling (*see* bullying: verbal)
National Administration Guidelines, 96
National Curriculum, 96, 97
Nuthall, G., 72, 97

Oliver M., 47, 74, 93

Palombaro, M. M., 10, 11, 12, 72, 97
Philips, R. J., 76
principals, 34, 39, 74, 95, 100
Purdue, K., 10, 45, 46, 47

Salisbury, C. L., 10, 11, 12, 72, 97
Sapon-Shevin, M., 10
Schleiffer, M., 84, 90, 91
school ethos, 47, 73, 74, 95-96, 98, 100

Schnorr, R., 10
Schwandt, T., 15
self-worth, 9
Sharp, S., 13
siblings, 51, 77, 83-92, 104
Skrtic T. M., 47
Smith, A., 8, 9, 10, 11
Smith, A. B., 73, 76, 94, 97
Smith, P. K., 12, 43
social relationships (*see also* environments), 7, 12, 15, 72, 94, 96-98, 101-104
special educational needs, 13
Strully, C., 10
Strully, J., 10
Sullivan, K., 7, 14, 19, 20, 43, 44, 49, 82

Taylor, S., 10, 47
teasing (*see* bullying: verbal)
threatening (*see* bullying: verbal)
Torrance, D. A., 12, 13
Traustadottir, R., 7, 70

United Nations Convention on the Rights of the Child (UNCROC), 100, 101
University of Otago Research and Ethics Committee, 8

vulnerability to abuse, 10, 20, 21, 43, 44

Whitney, I., 12, 13, 49

Zetlin, A., 11

for research & education
on intellectual disability

THE DONALD BEASLEY INSTITUTE is an independent, national, non-profit organisation governed by a Trust Board. The institute's aim is to advance the well-being of people in New Zealand with intellectual disabilities through applied research and education. The institute's goals include identifying critical issues affecting the lives of these people; undertaking and disseminating relevant research; and delivering evidence-based information, consultancy services, education, and training.

THE CHILDREN'S ISSUES CENTRE was established in 1995 by the University of Otago and the Children's Issues Trust to address matters that affect children and young people nationally, and to contribute to improving their well-being. In their work to date the Centre's key themes have been: children's experiences of family transitions; children and the law; young people's participation in schools and communities; and the quality of early childhood education.

OTHER TITLES AVAILABLE FROM NZCER

Caught Between Stories: Special Education in New Zealand
Dennis Moore, Angelika Anderson, Helen Timperley, Ted Glynn, Angus McFarlane, Don Brown, Charlotte Thomson
This review presents a thumbnail sketch of the history of special education. Two paradigms, or "stories", for conceptualising special education are described: the functional limitations paradigm, focusing on classification and remediation of individuals; and the ecological paradigm, focusing on the contribution of the environment to the learning and behaviour difficulties experienced by individuals.

The review concludes that an adequate understanding of learning or behaviour problems requires the examination of settings, behaviour, environmental events and goals. Several examples of assessment procedures developed in the ecological paradigm are identified. A discussion of successful intervention strategies is followed by consideration of the skills which the special educator requires, and the differing roles of parents, the broader community, and culture under the two paradigms.
NZCER 1999   ISBN 1-877140-58-9   Price: $18.00
Cat. No. 13268

Matauranga Motuhake Margaret Wilkie
Statistics show that Maori are over-represented in all negative indicators of special educational needs.

This report from NZCER, *Matauranga Motuhake,* is based on qualitative research that followed a kaupapa Maori process to present a uniquely Maori perspective on special education. The research shows the whanau as the main pillar supporting children with special educational needs. The examples given in the report show how some schools and services are able to offer successful support within a Maori kaupapa which is both Maori- and child-centred.

Matauranga Motuhake presents whanau-based responses where children are accepted and naturally integrated into their schools and communities. It can be argued that where whanau have access to services and support enabling their children to experience education on a par with other children, equitable solutions have been reached. The voices from each whanau are heard telling their own stories of the children as taonga, requiring extra special care or awhitanga, and the whanau strengthened by their experiences in the process.
NZCER 2001   ISBN 1-877140-60-0   Price: $36.00
Cat. No. 13294